ROCK REVIVAL

Y0-CAB-542

ISBN 0-634-00192-2

HAL•LEONARD®
CORPORATION
7777 W. BLUEMOUND RD. P.O. BOX 13819 MILWAUKEE, WI 53213

Visit Hal Leonard Online at
www.halleonard.com

RECORDED VERSIONS GUITAR ®

AUTHENTIC TRANSCRIPTIONS
WITH NOTES AND TABLATURE

ROCK REVIVAL

CONTENTS

INTRODUCTION

The Guess Who's "American Woman"

Derek and the Dominoes' "Layla"

Blue Oyster Cult's "Don't Fear the Reaper"

T. Rex's "Bang a Gong (Get It On)"

Bachman Turner Overdrive's "Let It Ride"

These songs are the rallying cry. They possess that indescribable rock energy that makes you shout and raise your fist in the air. They are the anthems of rock.

A driving beat, a killer guitar riff, and heartfelt passion are the key ingredients–common threads woven into the tapestry of each song. Their lyrics may speak of unrequited love, political unrest, or Dionysian revelry; still others will take you on a mystical journey.
Whether it's a soundtrack to a memory or the reason for the memory itself, music that changes you is as important to any other influence or event in you life. These are points in time that are unshakeable, and the songs that define them are our own personal anthems. No matter what the theme, they make you feel that you are there.

Rock 'n' roll is a force so determined to be original that its disciples don't often admit how strongly they've been influenced by musicians and bands of the past. There can be little doubt, however, that the songs included in this book rank as both rock classics and musical standards. This collection contains twenty gems from a golden age of guitar rock, 1967-1976. Each has withstood the ultimate test of time.

American Woman

**Written by Burton Cummings, Randy Bachman,
Gary Peterson and Jim Kale**

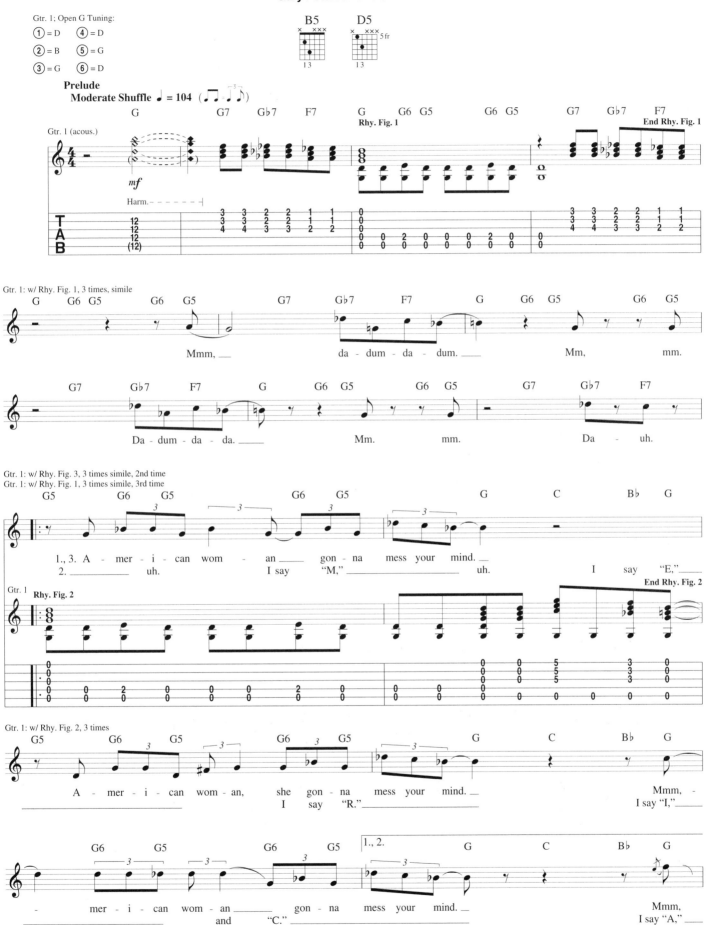

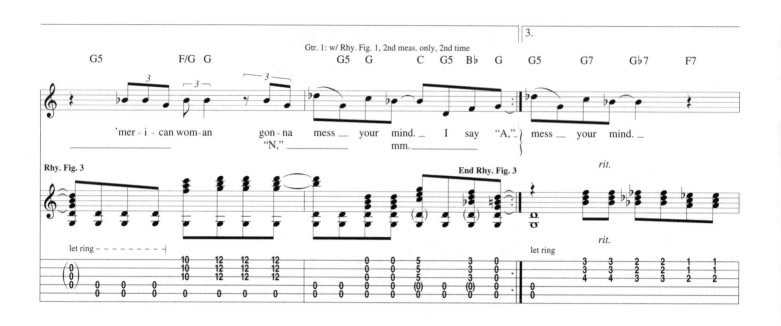

'mer - i - can wom-an   gon - na   mess ___ your mind. ___ I   say "A,"   mess ___ your mind. ___
"N," ___   mm. ___

Intro
Moderate Rock ♩ = 88

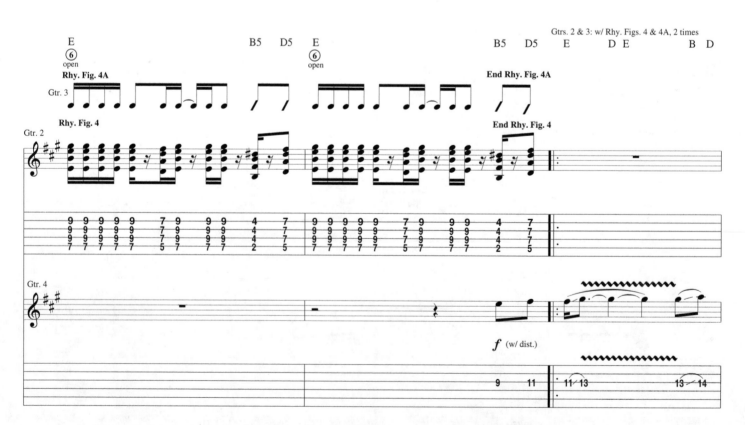

Gtr. 4: w/ Fill 1, 1st time
Gtr. 4: w/ Fill 3, 2nd time

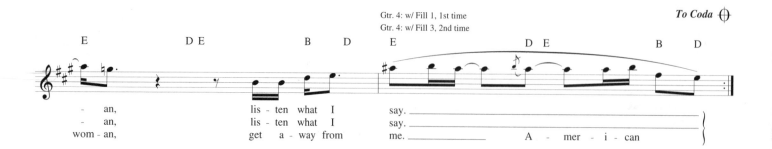

‑ an,   lis - ten what I   say. ___
‑ an,   lis - ten what I   say. ___
wom - an,   get a - way from   me. ___ A - mer - i - can

Guitar Solo

Gtrs. 2 & 3: w/ Rhy. Figs. 4 & 4A, 8 times, simile

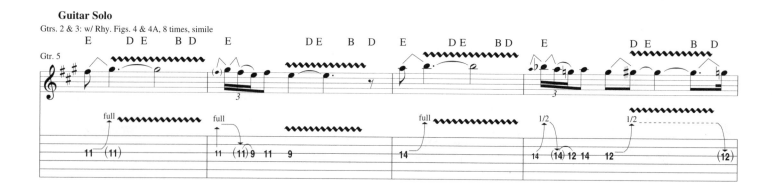

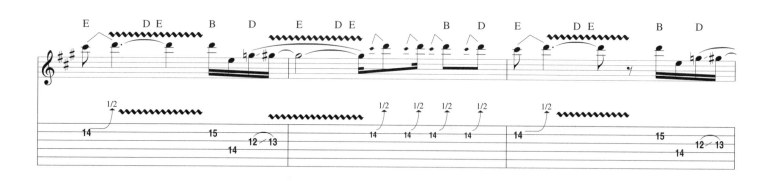

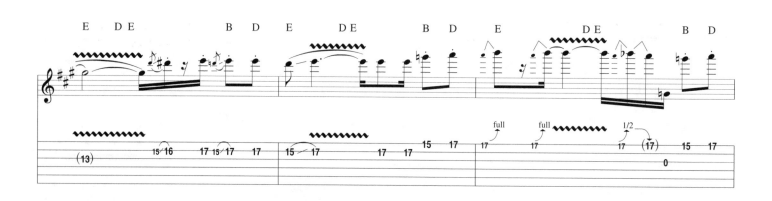

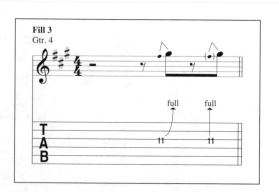

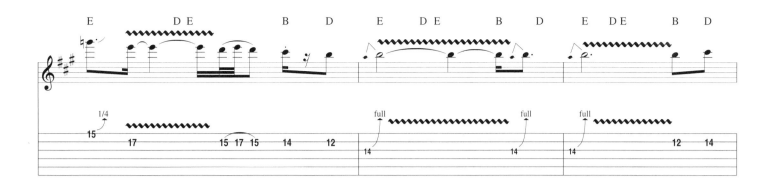

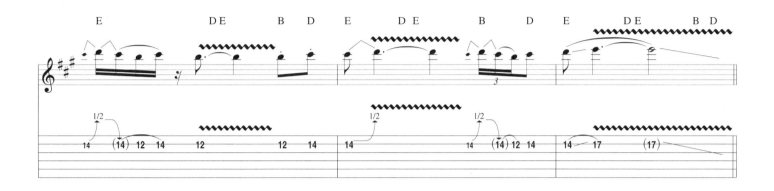

Interlude
Gtr. 4 tacet

Gtrs. 2 & 3

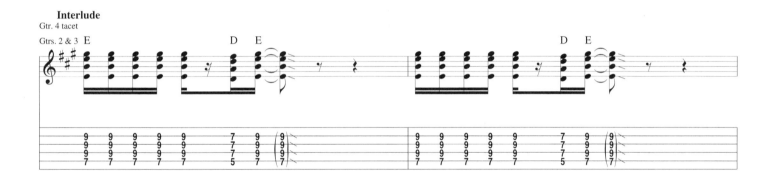

D.S. al Coda

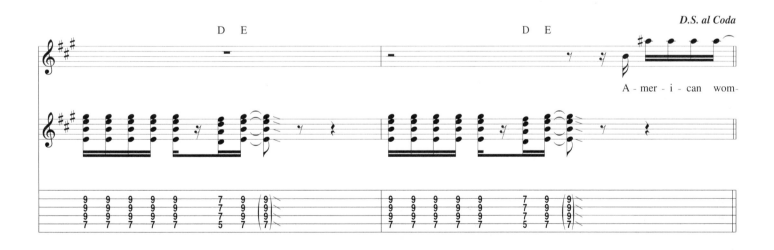

A - mer - i - can wom-

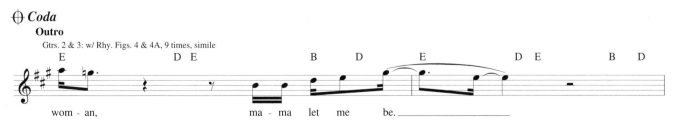

⊕ Coda
Outro

Gtrs. 2 & 3: w/ Rhy. Figs. 4 & 4A, 9 times, simile

wom - an,   ma - ma let me be._____

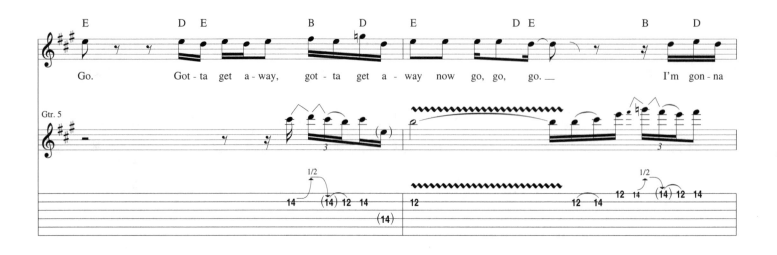

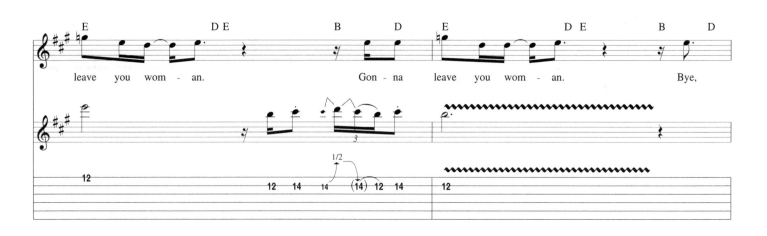

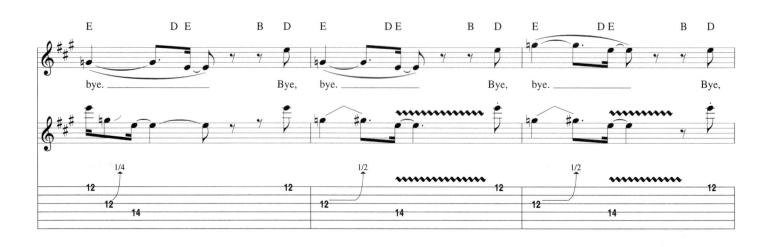

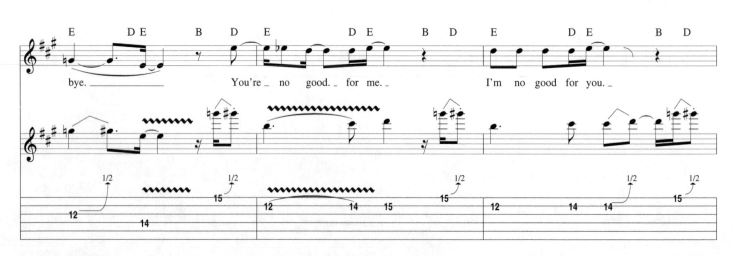

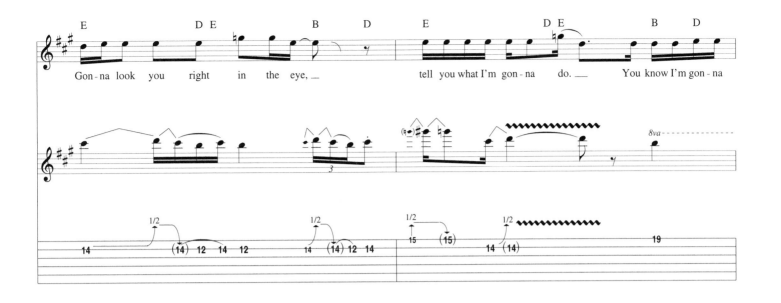

Gon - na look you right in the eye, ___ tell you what I'm gon - na do. ___ You know I'm gon - na

leave. You know I'm gon - na go. You know I'm gon - na

Fade Out

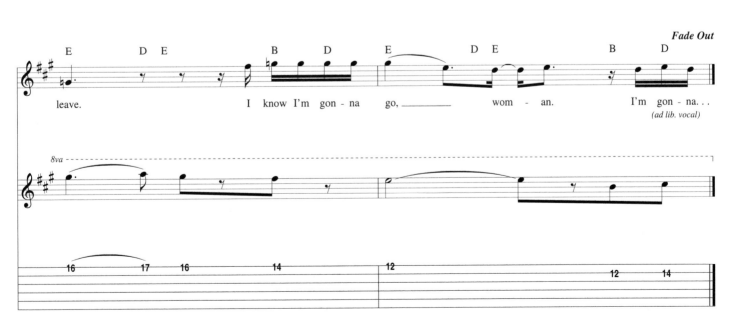

leave. I know I'm gon - na go, _____ wom - an. I'm gon - na...

(ad lib. vocal)

Bang a Gong (Get It On)

Words and Music by Marc Bolan

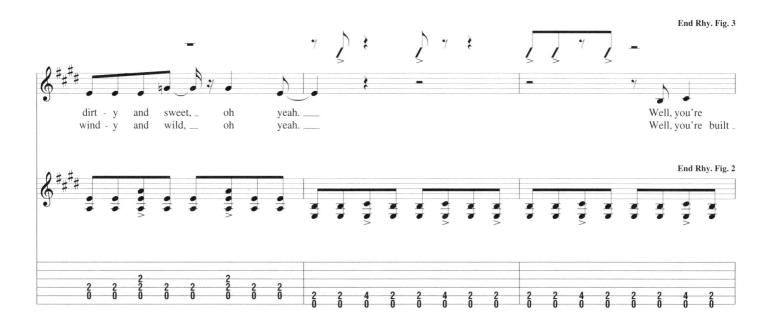

End Rhy. Fig. 2

dirt - y and sweet, oh yeah. _____ Well, you're
wind - y and wild, oh yeah. _____ Well, you're built _

Gtrs. 1 & 2: w/ Rhy. Fig. 2, simile
Gtr. 3 tacet

Gtr. 3: w/ Rhy. Fig. 3, 1st time

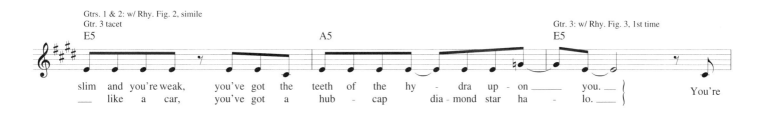

E5   A5   E5

slim and you're weak, you've got the teeth of the hy - dra up - on _____ you. _____ You're
_____ like a car, you've got a hub - cap dia - mond star ha - lo. _____

Gtr. 3: w/ Rhy. Fig. 3, last two meas., 2nd time

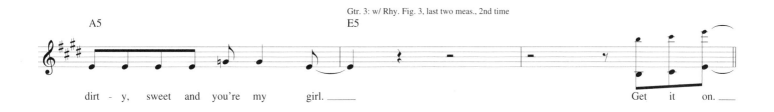

A5   E5

dirt - y, sweet and you're my girl. _____ Get it on. _____

Chorus

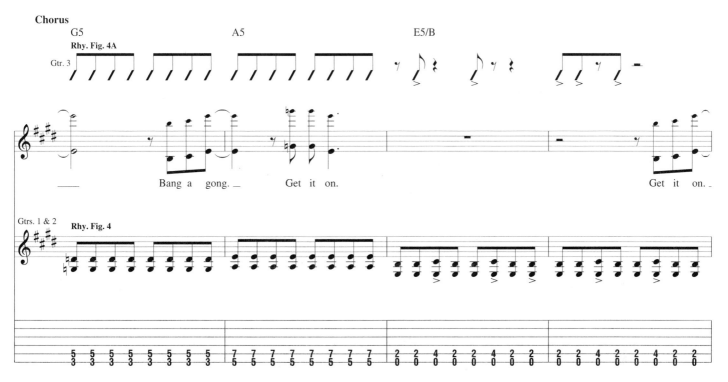

G5   A5   E5/B

Rhy. Fig. 4A
Gtr. 3

_____ Bang a gong. _____ Get it on.   Get it on. _

Gtrs. 1 & 2
Rhy. Fig. 4

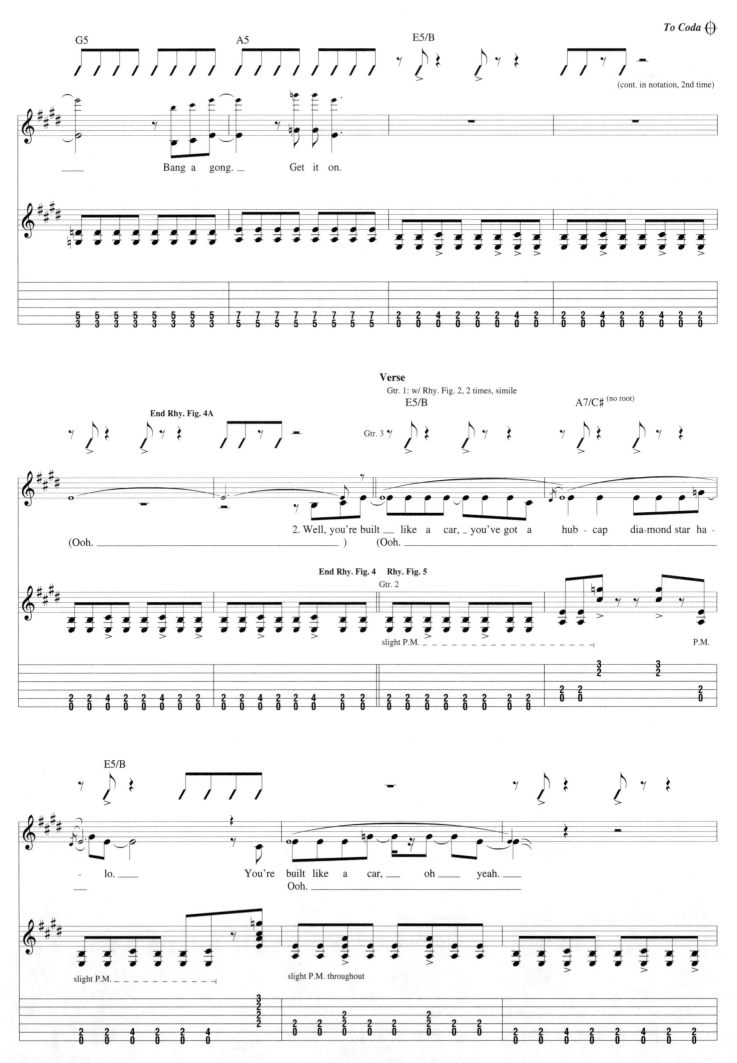

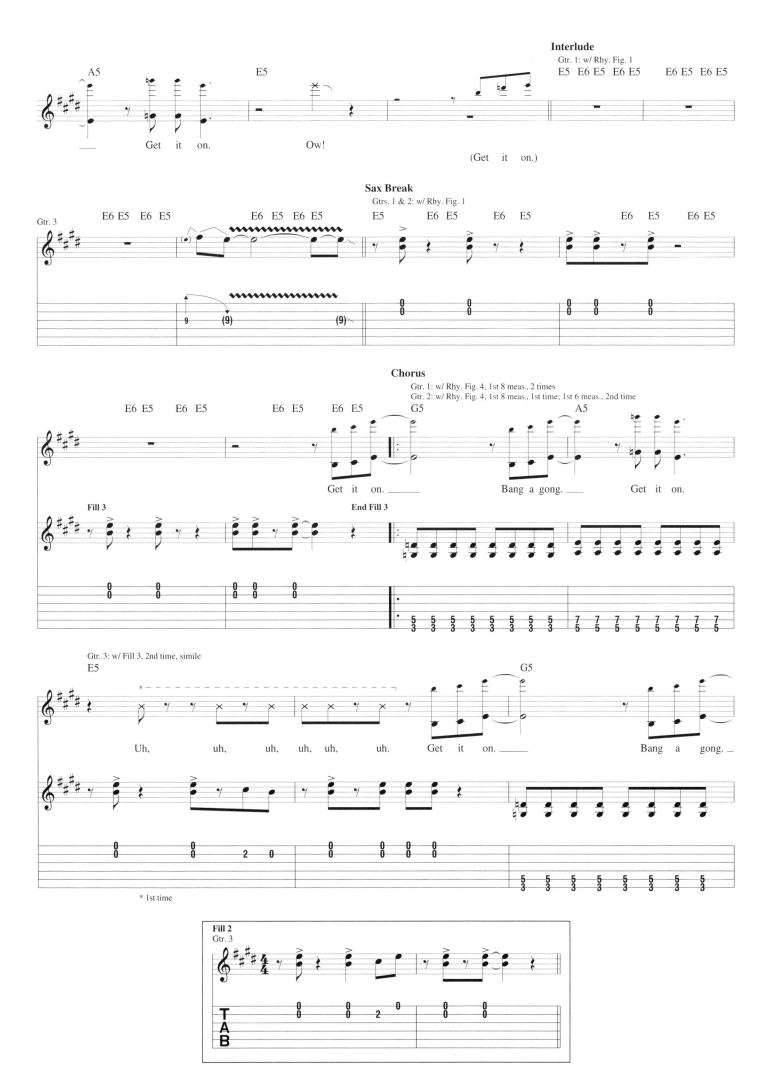

Can't You See

Words and Music by Toy Caldwell

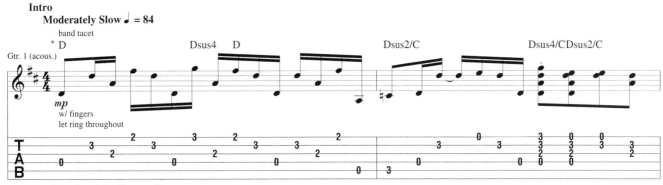

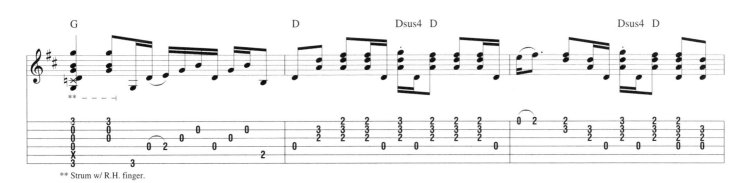

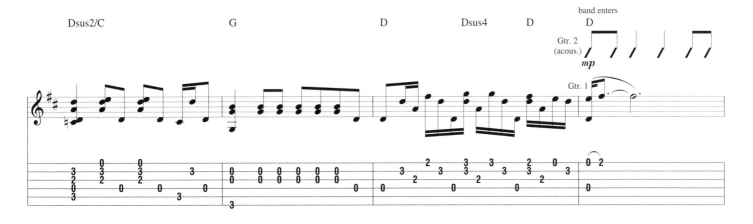

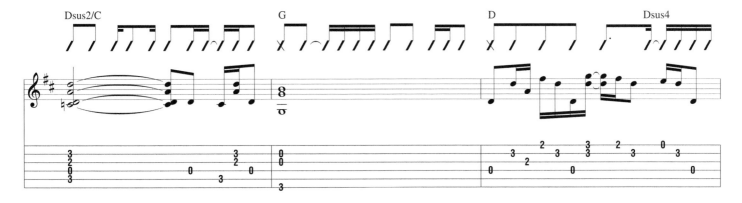

* played w/ thumb

the high-est moun-tain. I jump off, no-bod-y gon-na know.

Chorus

Can't you see, ___ whoa,

can't you see ___ what that wom-an, Lord, ___ she been do-in' to me? ___

Can't you see, ____ can't you see ___

what that wo-man, she been do-in' to me? ___

Guitar Solo
Gtr. 1: w/ Rhy. Fig. 4, 1 1/2 times, simile
Gtr. 2: w/ Rhy. Fig. 1, simile

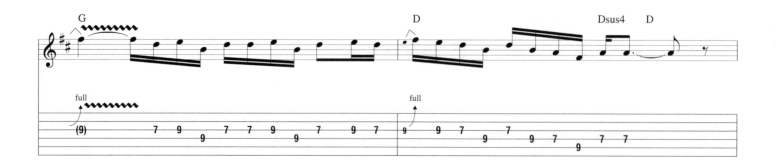

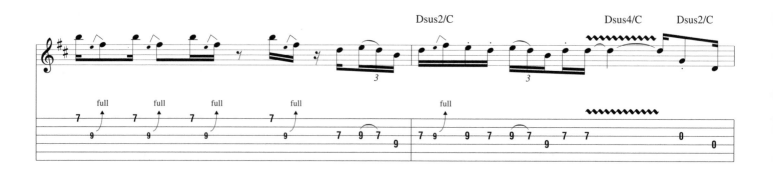

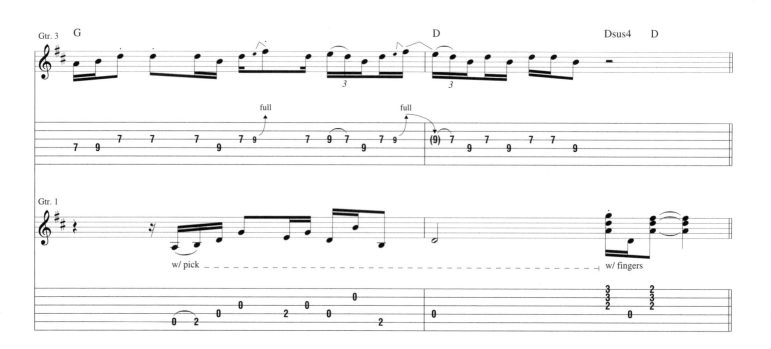

Verse

Gtrs. 1 & 2: w/ Rhy. Figs. 2 & 2A, simile

3. I'm gon-na buy a tick-et, now, as far as I can. Ain't nev-er comin' back.

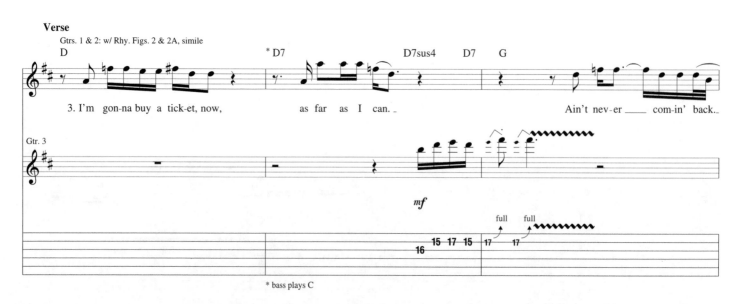

* bass plays C

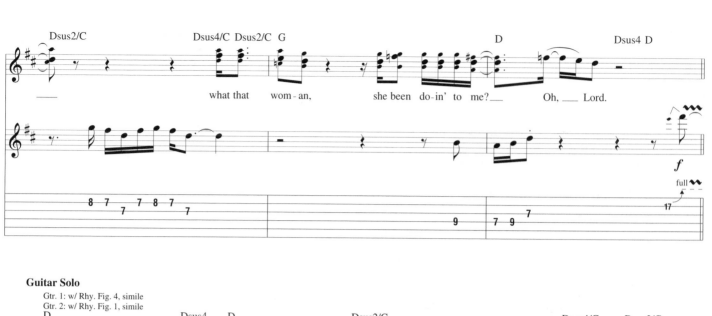

what that wom-an, she been do-in' to me?___ Oh, ___ Lord.

Guitar Solo

Gtr. 1: w/ Rhy. Fig. 4, simile
Gtr. 2: w/ Rhy. Fig. 1, simile

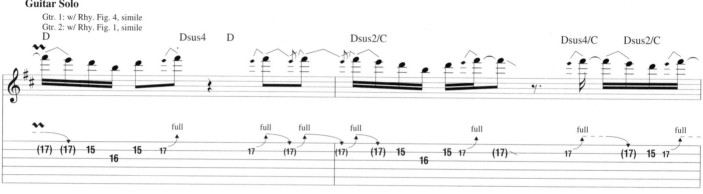

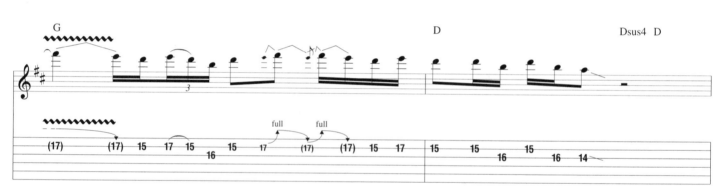

Can't you

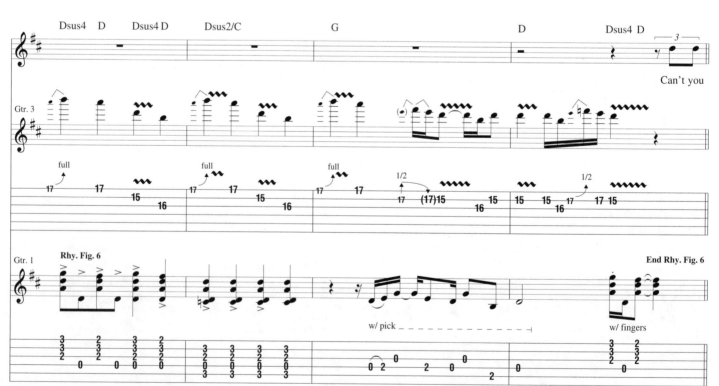

*Played ahead of the beat.

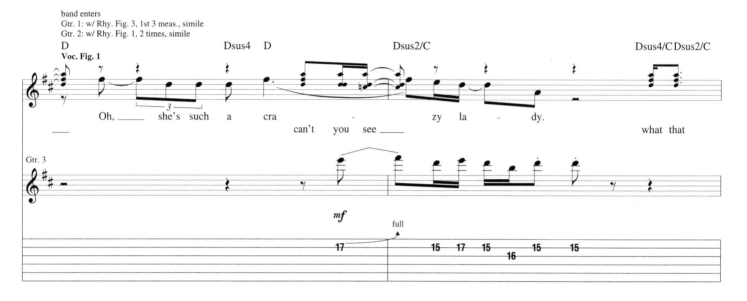

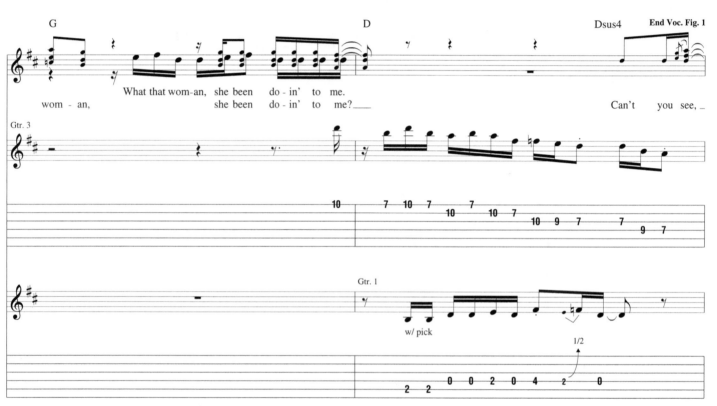

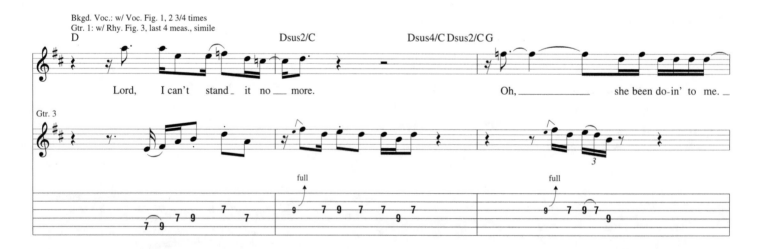

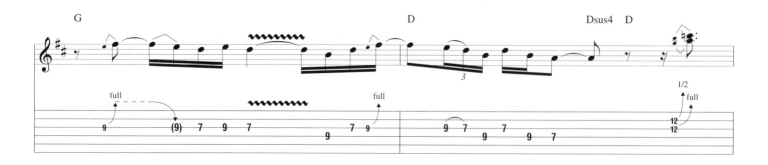

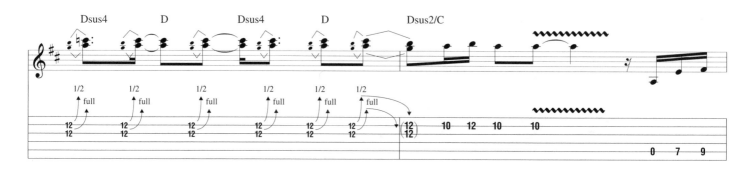

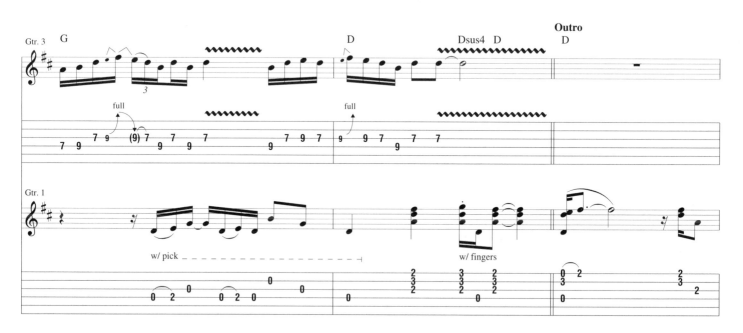

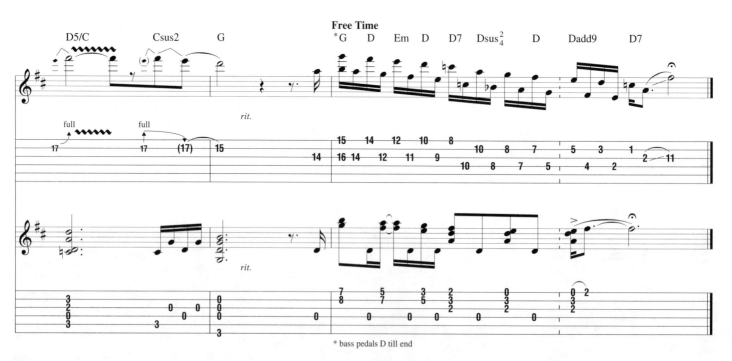

* bass pedals D till end

Carry on Wayward Son

Words and Music by Kerry Livgren

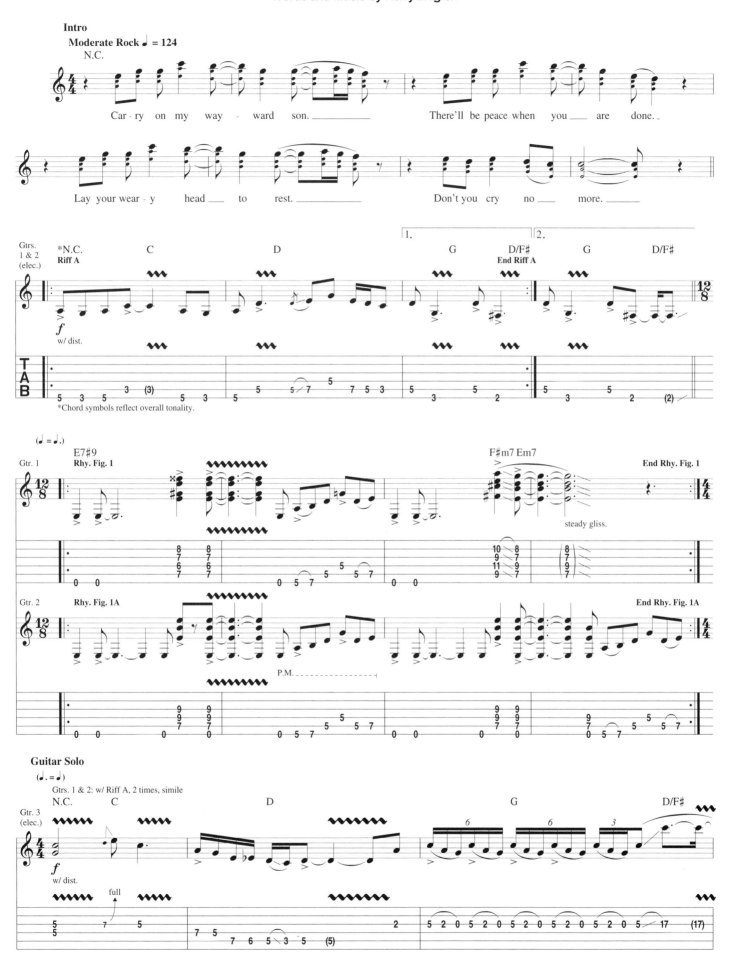

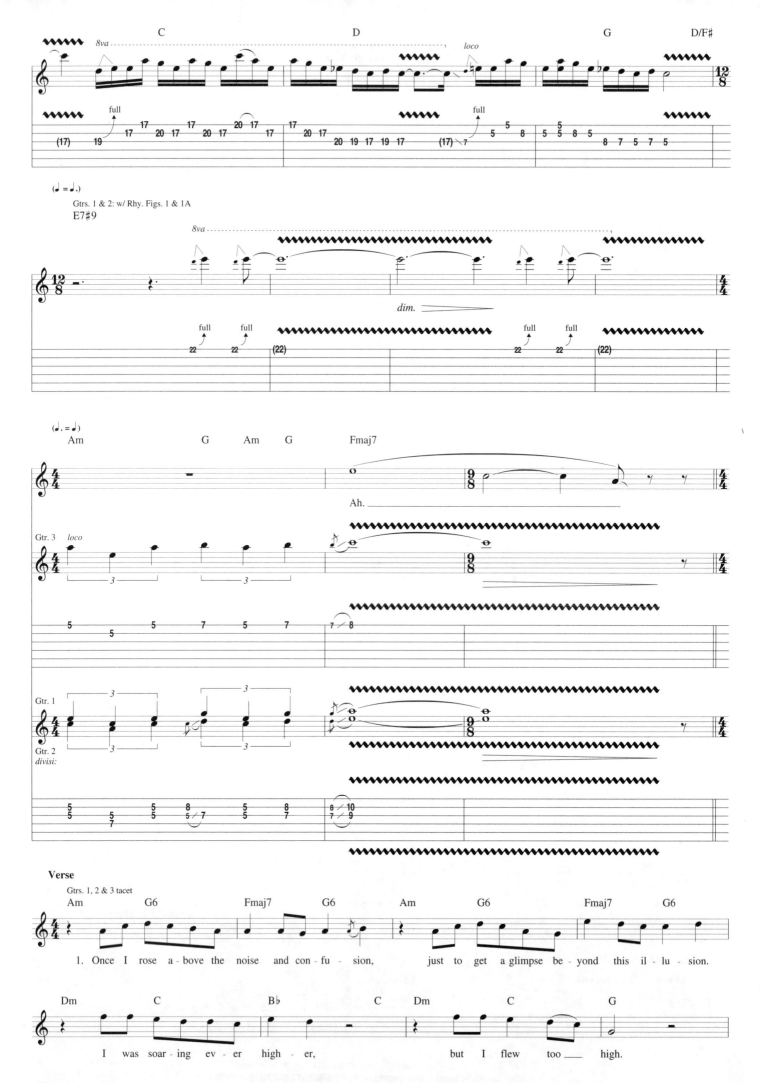

Verse

Gtrs. 1, 2 & 3 tacet

1. Once I rose a-bove the noise and con-fu-sion, just to get a glimpse be-yond this il-lu-sion.

I was soar-ing ev-er high-er, but I flew too ___ high.

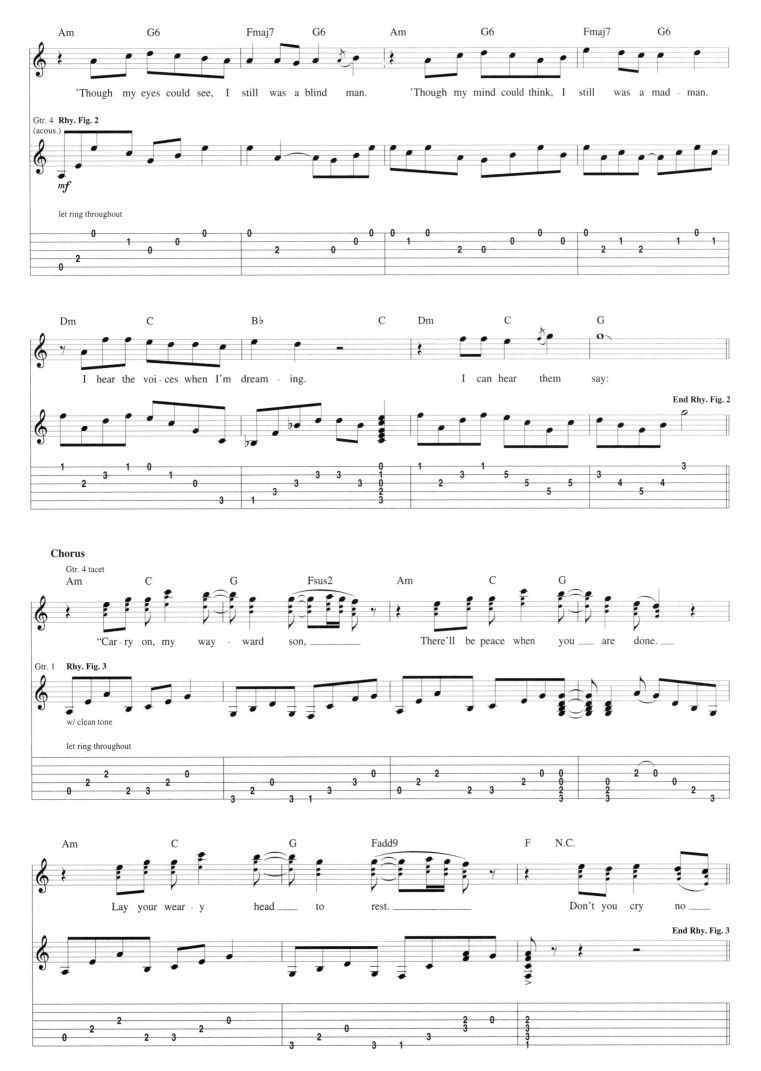

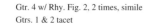

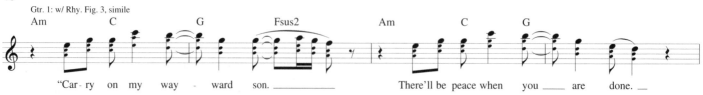

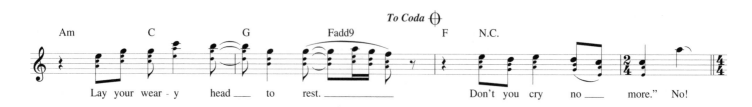

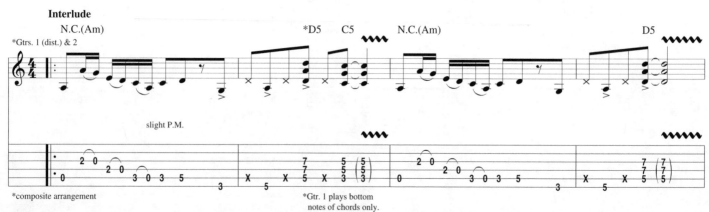

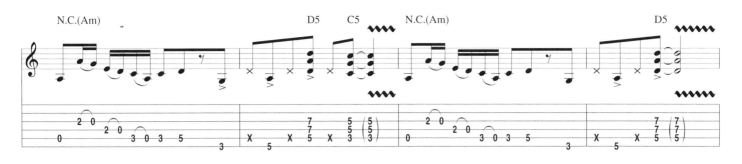

1.

Organic Solo

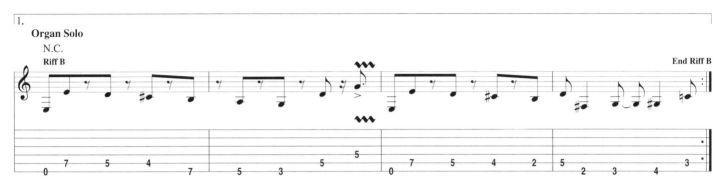

2.

Guitar Solo

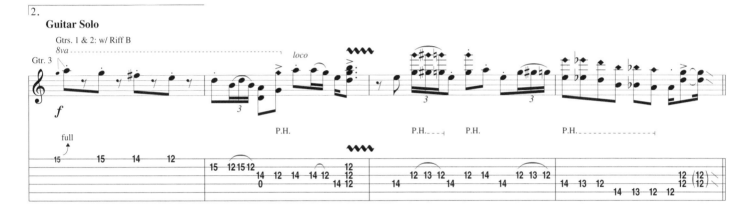

Interlude

Bridge

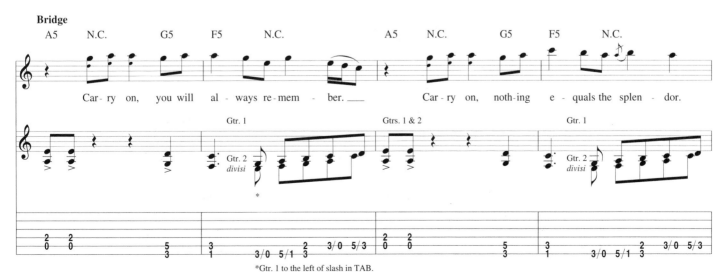

Car - ry on, you will al - ways re - mem - ber. ___ Car - ry on, noth-ing e - quals the splen - dor.

*Gtr. 1 to the left of slash in TAB.

Come Together

Words and Music by John Lennon and Paul McCartney

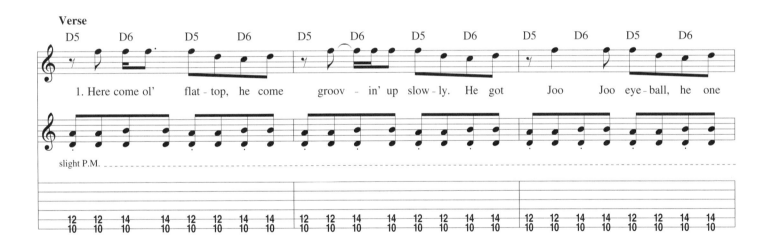

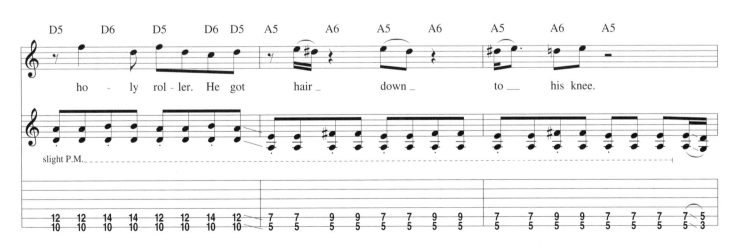

Guitar Solo

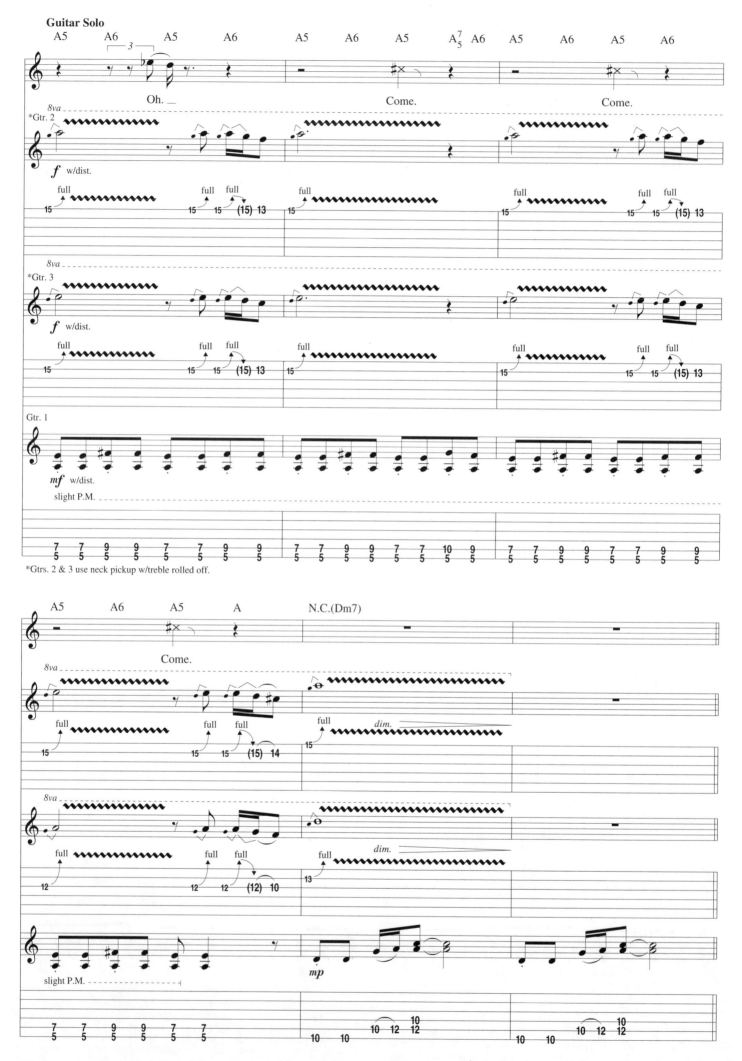

*Gtrs. 2 & 3 use neck pickup w/treble rolled off.

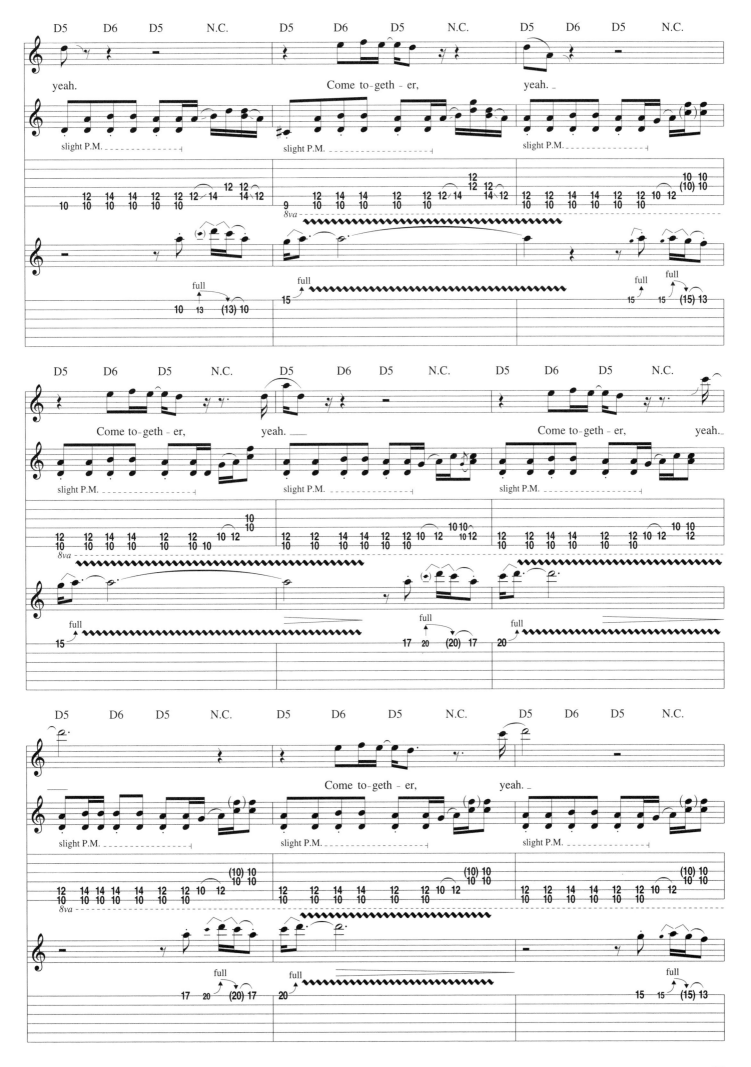

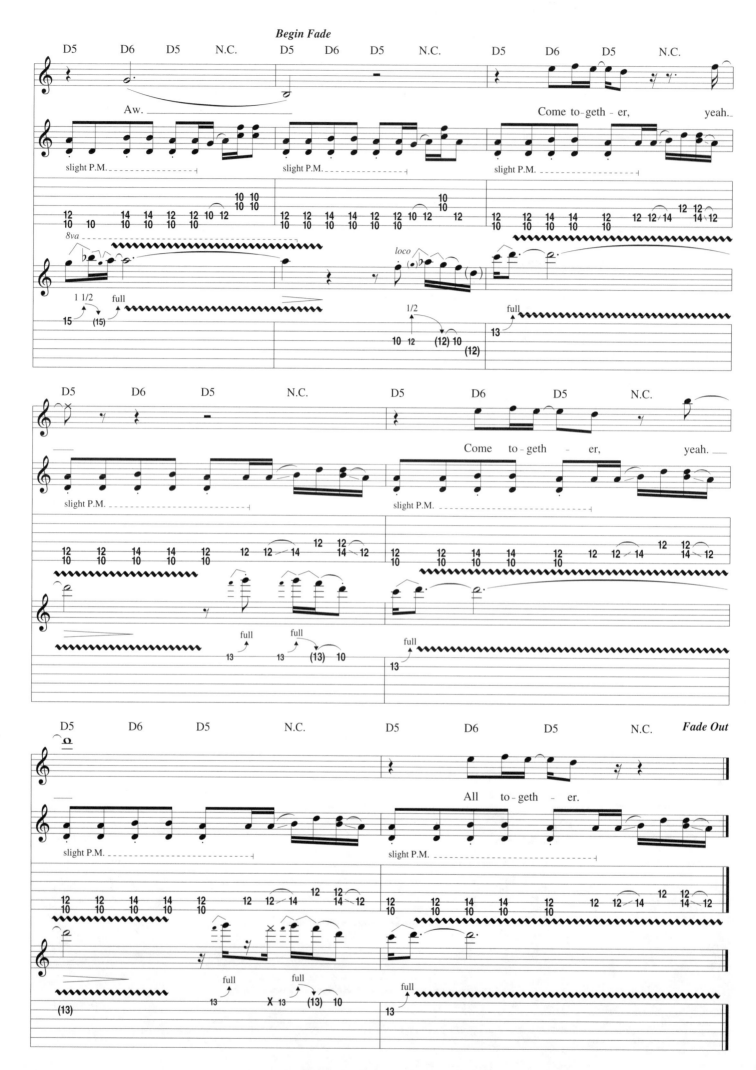

Don't Fear the Reaper

Words and Music by Donald Roeser

-er. Ba - by take my hand. Don't fear the reap - er. We'll be a - ble to fly. Don't fear the reap -

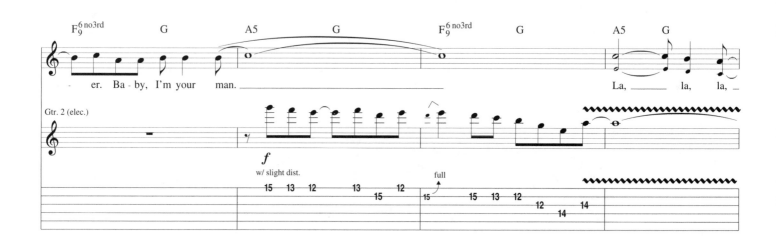

-er. Ba - by, I'm your man. La, la, la,

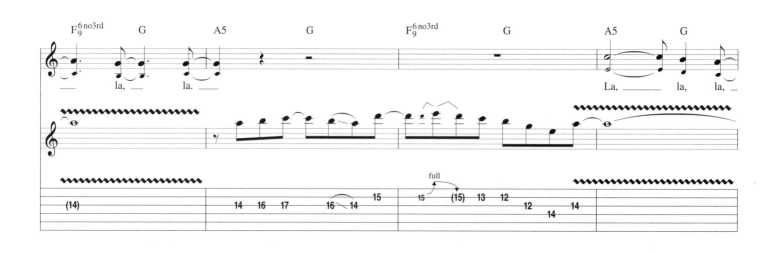

la, la. La, la, la,

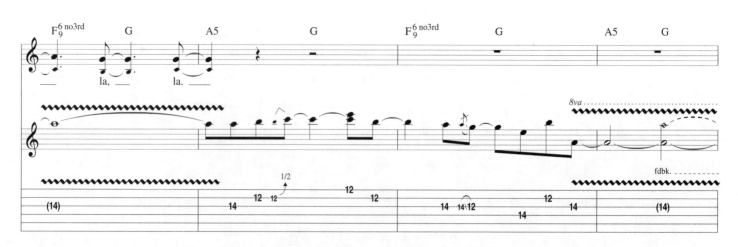

la, la.

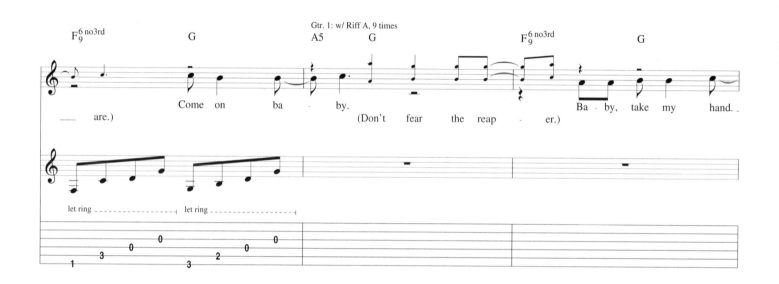

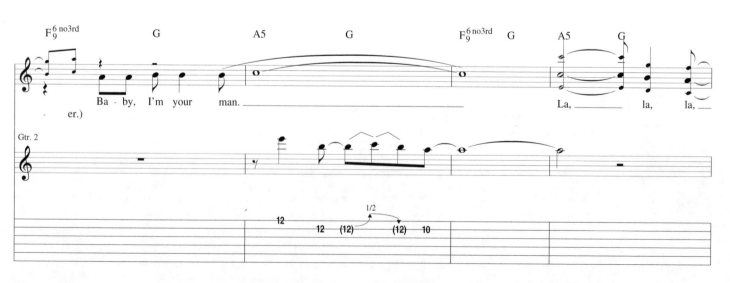

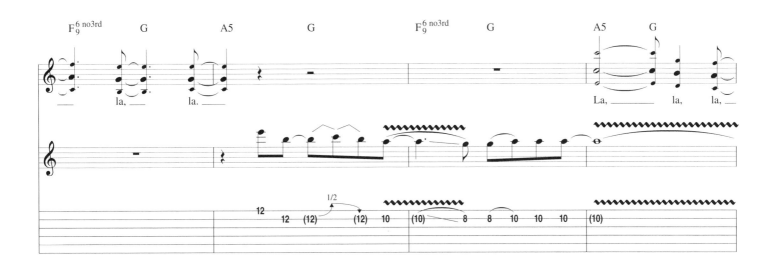

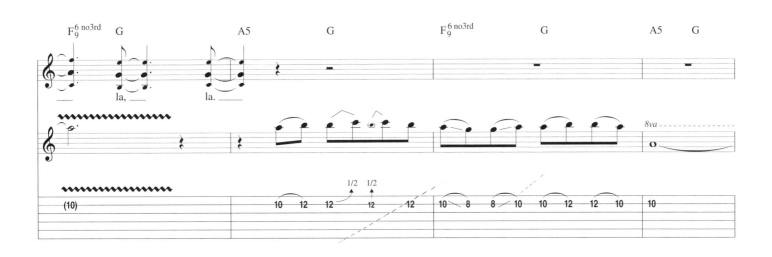

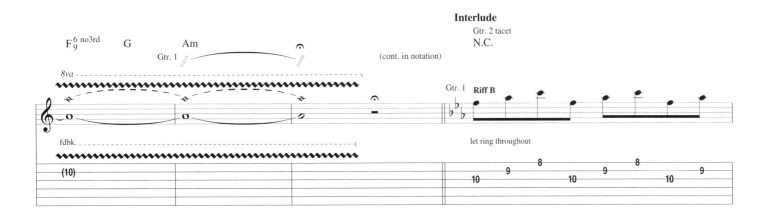

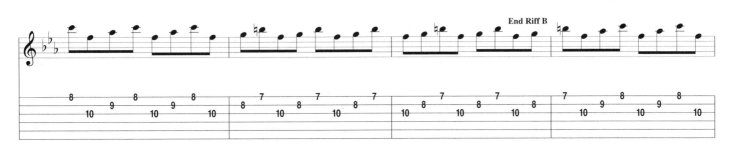

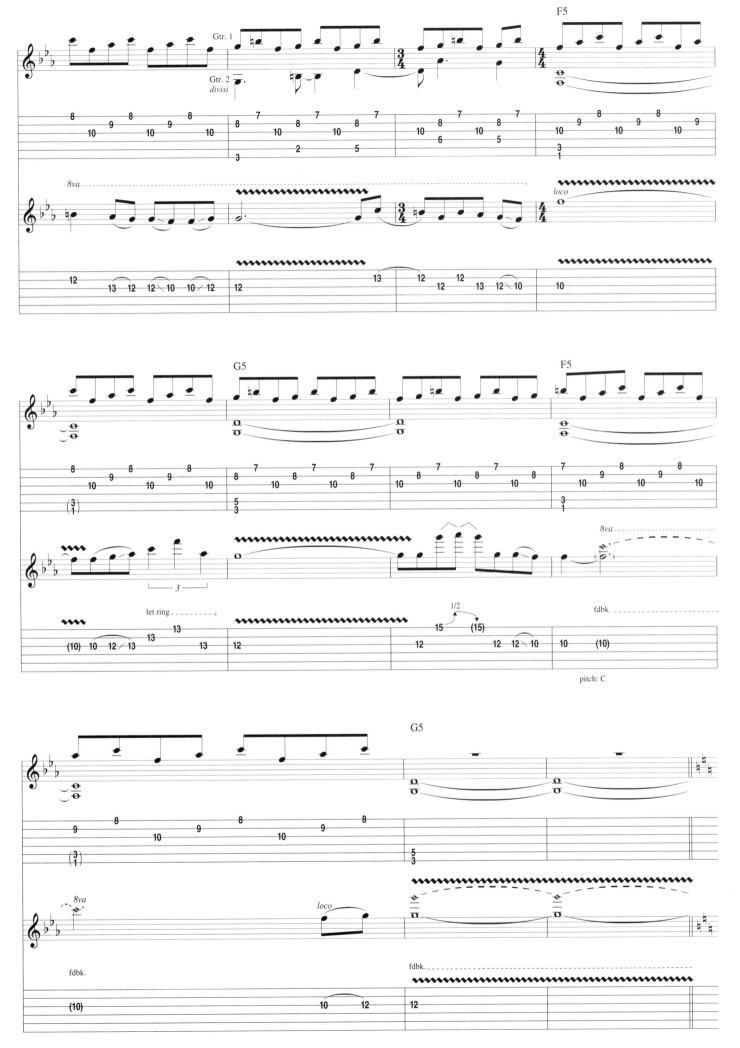

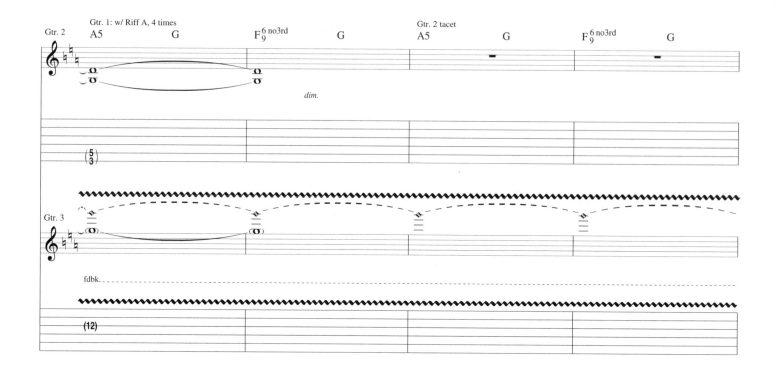

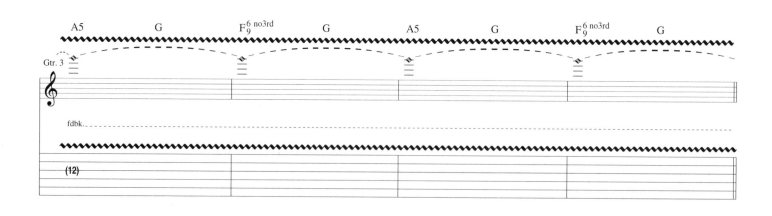

Verse

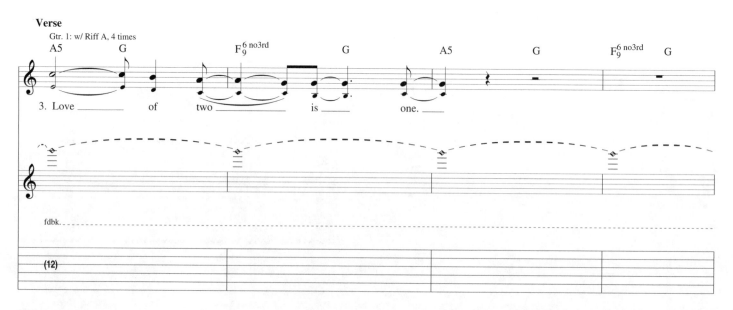

3. Love _____ of two _____ is _____ one. _____

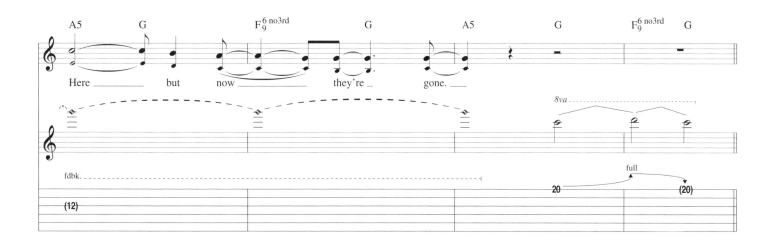

Here _____ but now _____ they're ____ gone. _____

Chorus

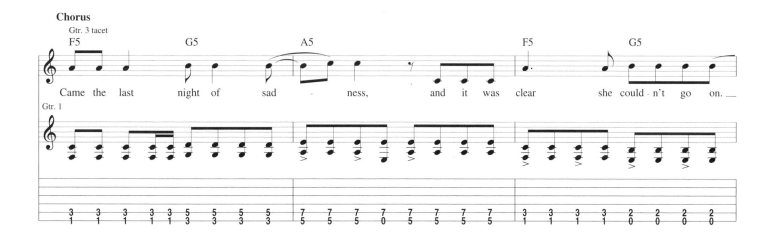

Came the last night of sad - ness, and it was clear she could-n't go on. ____

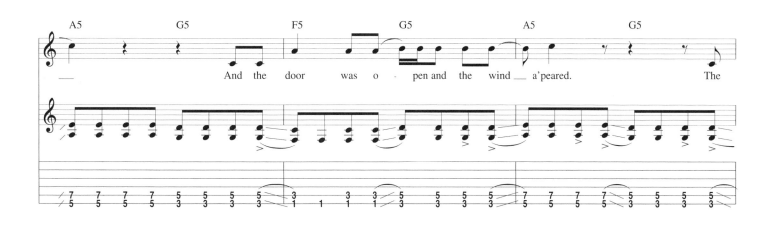

___ And the door was o - pen and the wind ___ a'peared. The

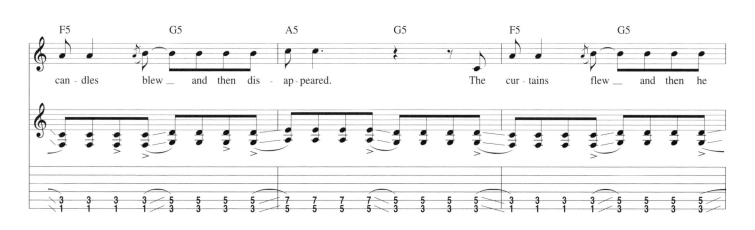

can - dles blew __ and then dis - ap-peared. The cur - tains flew __ and then he

57

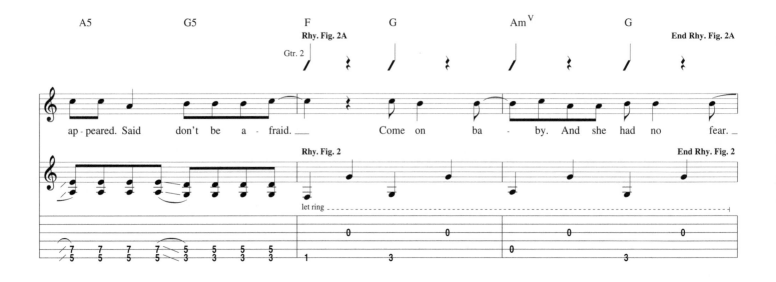

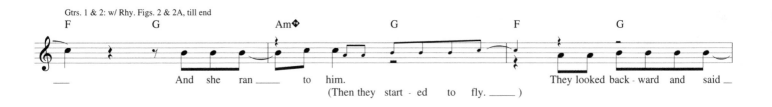

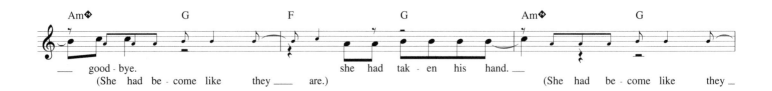

*Two gtrs. arr. for one.

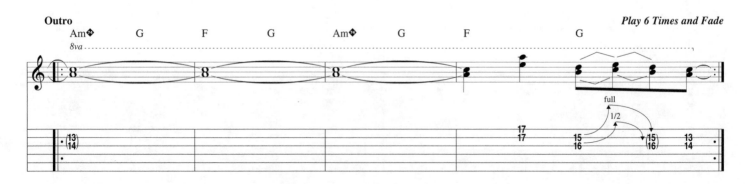

Green-Eyed Lady

Words and Music by Jerry Corbetta, J.C. Phillips and David Riordan

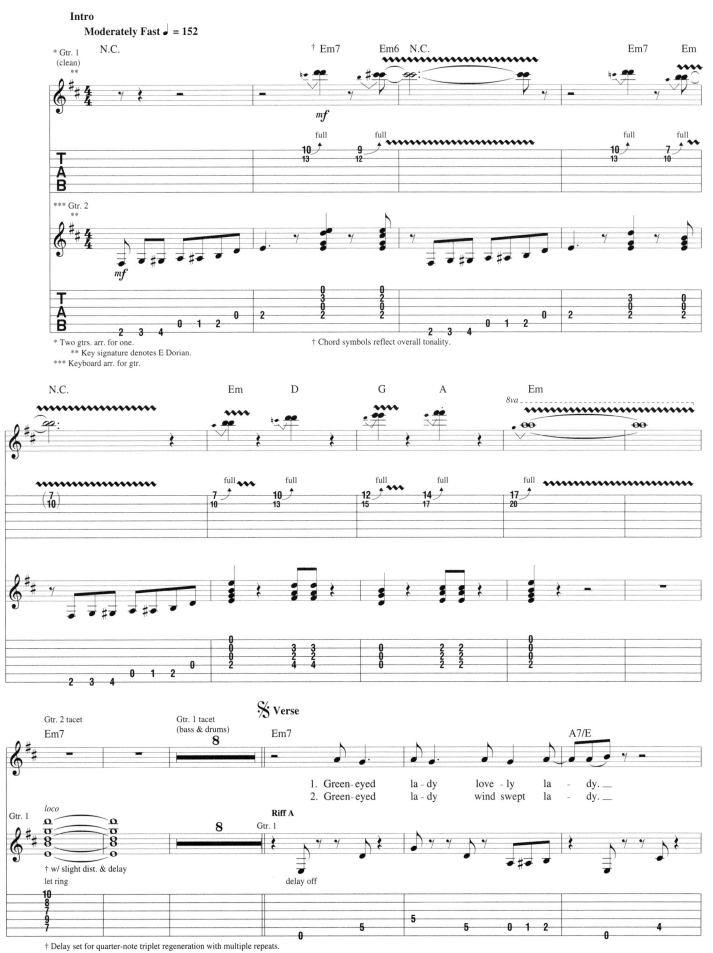

* Two gtrs. arr. for one.
  ** Key signature denotes E Dorian.
*** Keyboard arr. for gtr.

† Chord symbols reflect overall tonality.

† Delay set for quarter-note triplet regeneration with multiple repeats.

Hey Joe

Words and Music by Billy Roberts

you know I caught her mess-in' 'round with an-oth-er man.

Yeah!

Ooh.

I'm go-in' down to shoot my old la-dy,

you know I caught her mess-in' 'round   with an - oth-er man. __   Huh!   And   that ain't

too   cool.
__)

2. Uh, hey, __ Joe, __   I heard you. shot your

(Ah. _____

woman down, you shot her down, now.

Uh, hey, ___ Joe,

Ah. ___

I heard you shot your old

la - dy down, ___ you shot her down in the ground. ___ Yeah! ___

Yes, I ___ did, I shot her, you know I caught her mess - in' 'round,
Ah. _____

mess-in' 'round town. ___

Uh, yes I did, I shot her, you know I caught my old la-dy mess-in' 'round

Ah. ___

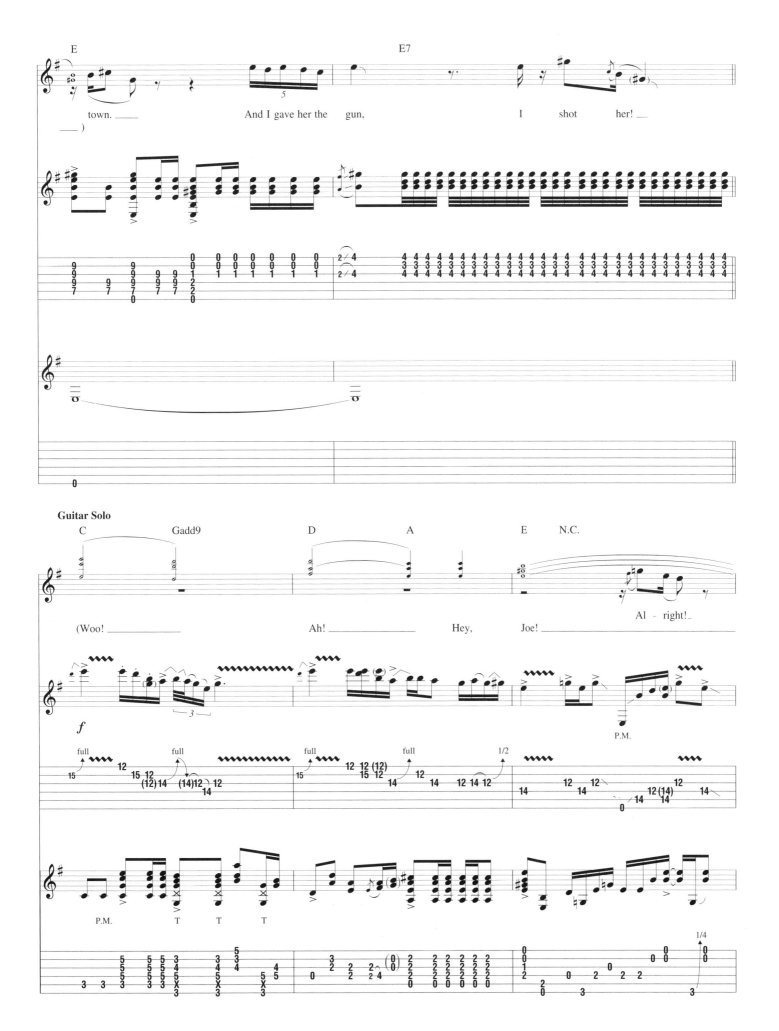

way down _____ where I _____ can be free! Ain't no one _____

Joe, where you gon - na go? _____

_____ gon-na find me babe!

Hey, _____ Ain't no hang - man gon-na,

Hot Blooded

Words and Music by Mick Jones and Lou Gramm

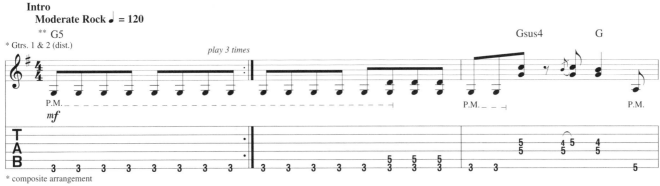

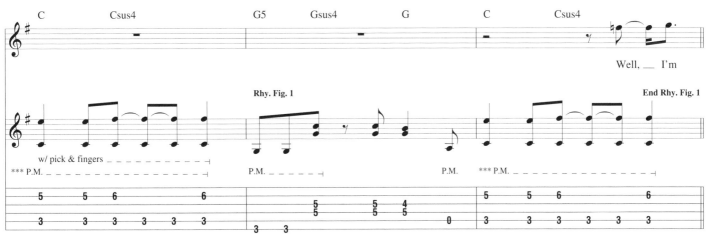

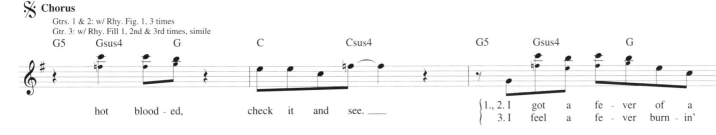

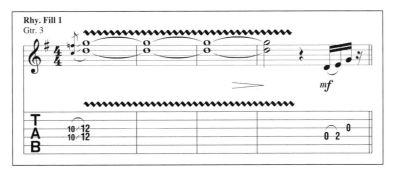

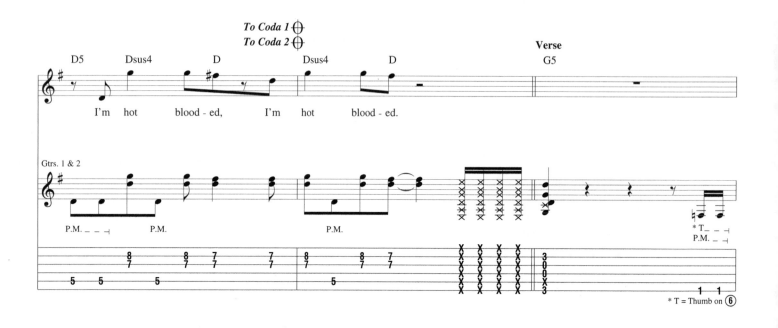

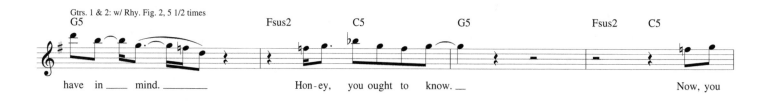

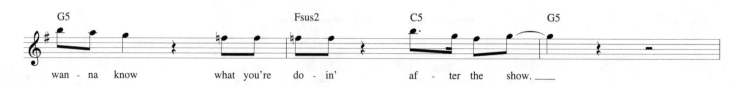

all ___ right, ___ may-be you can stay ___ all ___ night. ___

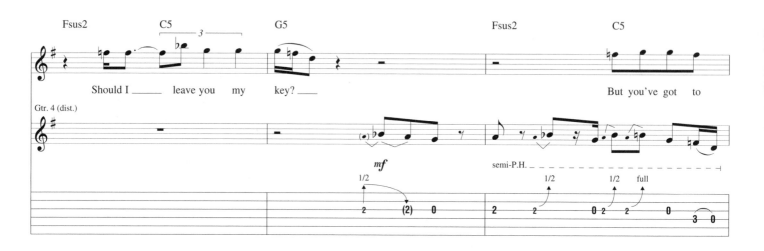

Should I ___ leave you my key? ___ But you've got to

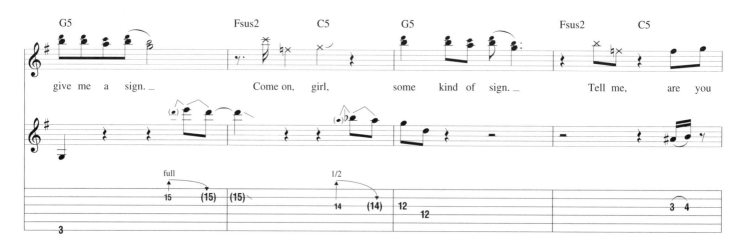

give me a sign. ___ Come on, girl, some kind of sign. ___ Tell me, are you

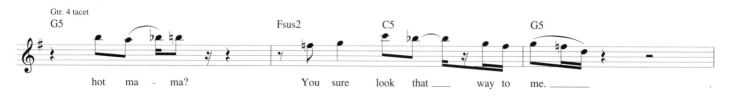

hot ma-ma? You sure look that ___ way to me. ___

Pre-Chorus

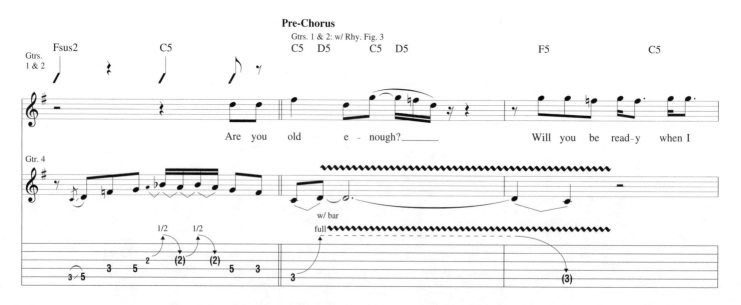

Are you old e-nough? ___ Will you be read-y when I

x

x

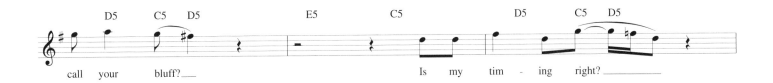

call your bluff? ___ Is my tim - ing right? _____

D.S. al Coda 2
Gtr. 3: w/ Rhy. Fig. 3, last meas.

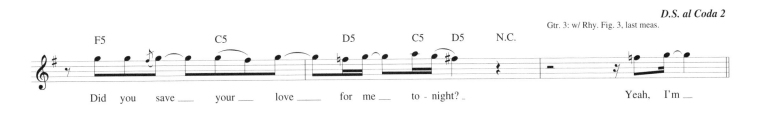

Did you save ___ your ___ love ___ for me ___ to - night? ___ Yeah, I'm ___

Coda 2

Guitar Solo
Gtrs. 1 & 2: w/ Rhy. Fig. 2, 7 1/2 times

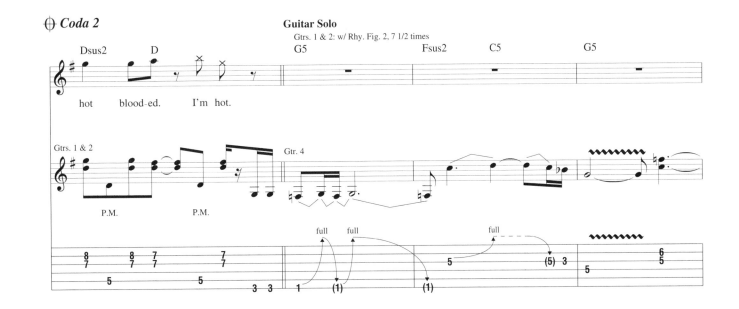

hot blood-ed. I'm hot.

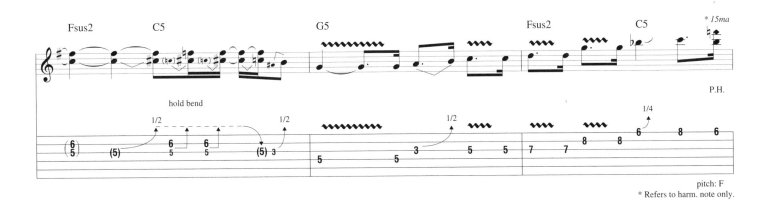

pitch: F
* Refers to harm. note only.

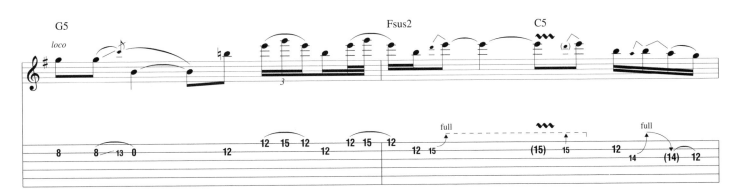

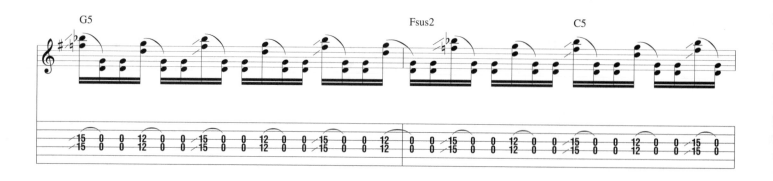

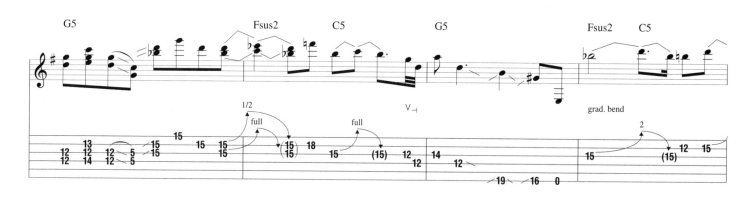

Pre-Chorus

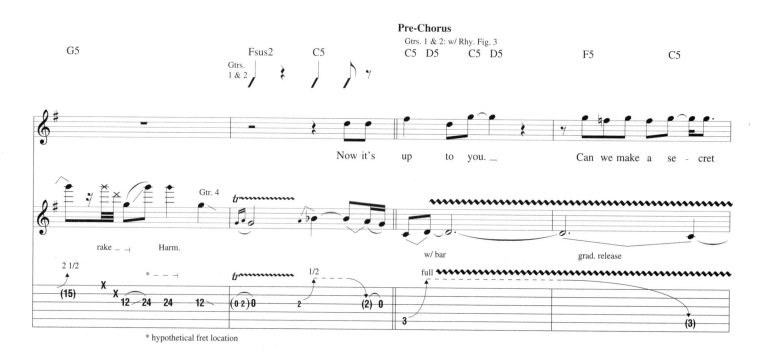

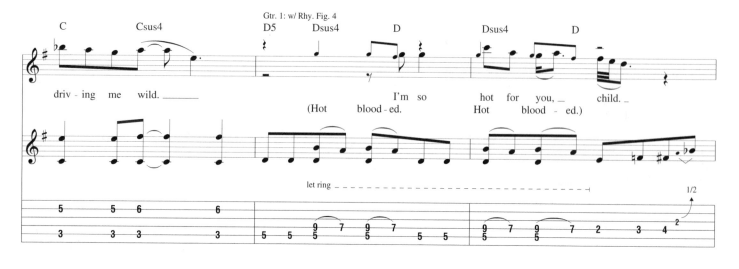

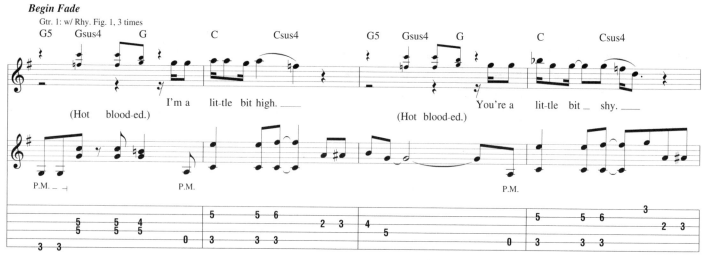

Layla

Words and Music by Eric Clapton and Jim Gordon

* Composite arr. Gtr. 6 mixed down on this recording. It is easier to hear on previous releases.

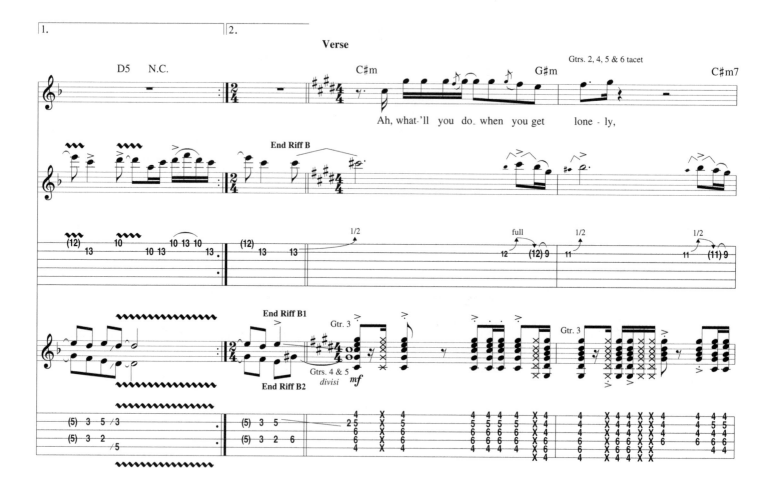

Verse

Gtrs. 2, 4, 5 & 6 tacet

Ah, what-'ll you do_ when you get lone - ly,

End Riff B

End Riff B1

End Riff B2

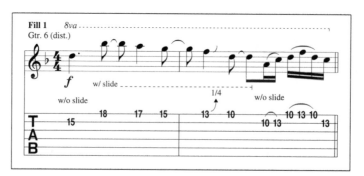

Fill 1
Gtr. 6 (dist.)

Rhy. Fill 1
Gtr. 3

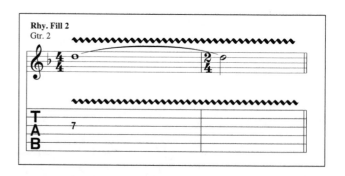

Rhy. Fill 2
Gtr. 2

Fill 2
Gtr. 6

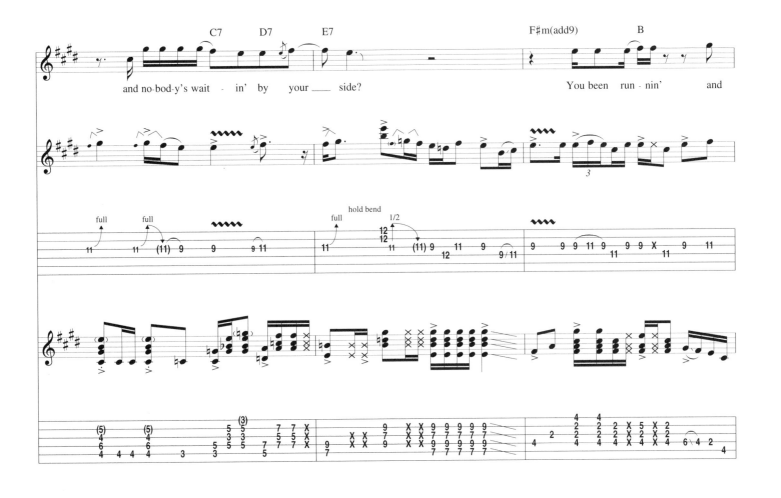

and no-bod-y's wait - in' by your ___ side?   You been run - nin'   and

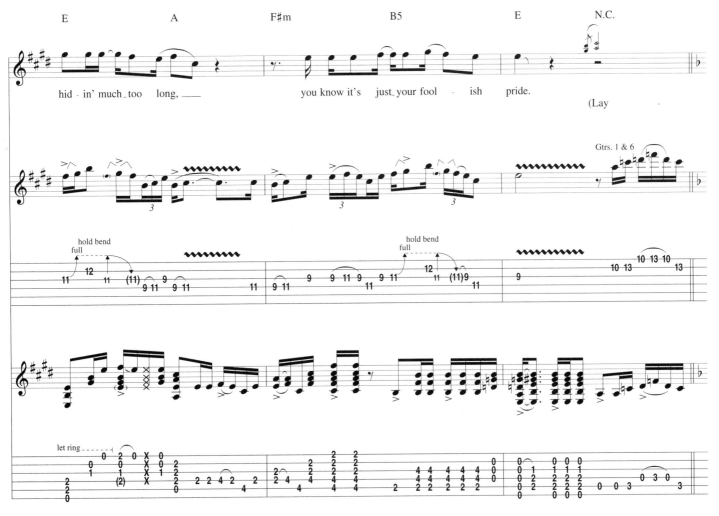

hid - in' much_too   long, ___   you know it's   just_your fool - ish   pride.

(Lay

ℑ Chorus

Gtrs. 1, 4 & 5: w/ Riffs B, B1 & B2, 1st & 2nd times;
             w/ Riffs B, B1 & B2, 1st 7 meas, 3rd time
Gtr. 2: w/ Riff A, 3 times
Gtr. 3: w/ Rhy. Fig. 1, 3 times
Gtr. 6: w/ Fill 3, 1st time; w/ Riff B, 1st 4 meas, 2nd time;
             w/ Riff B, 1st 2 meas., 3rd time

la. _____

You got me on ___ my knees. _

Lay - la. _____)

I

88

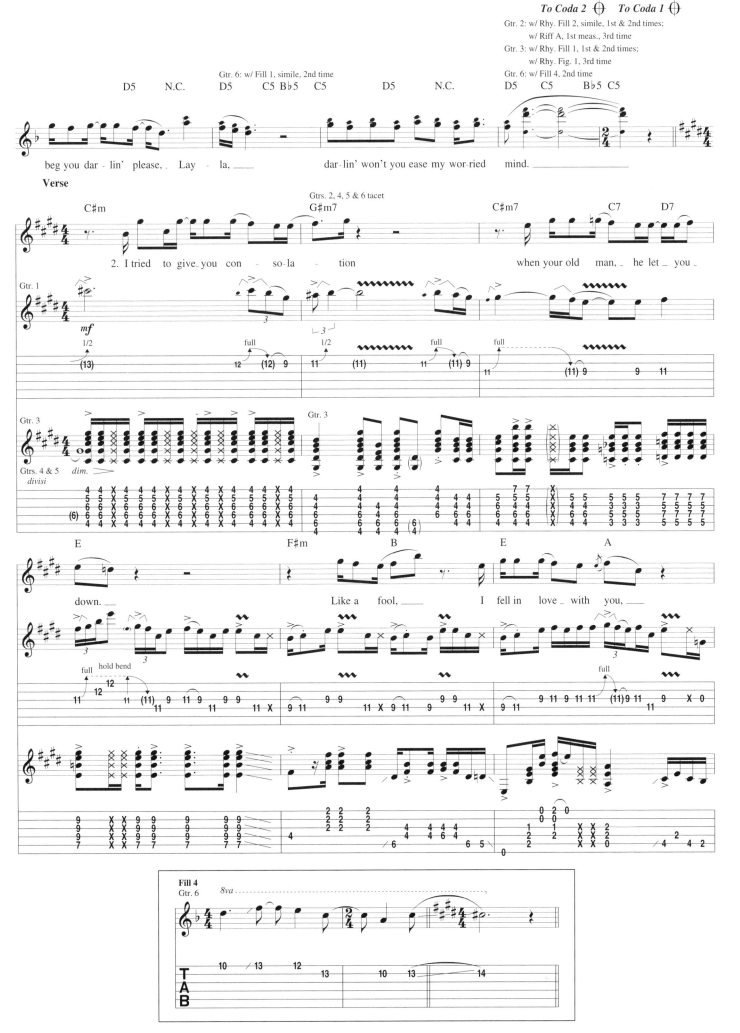

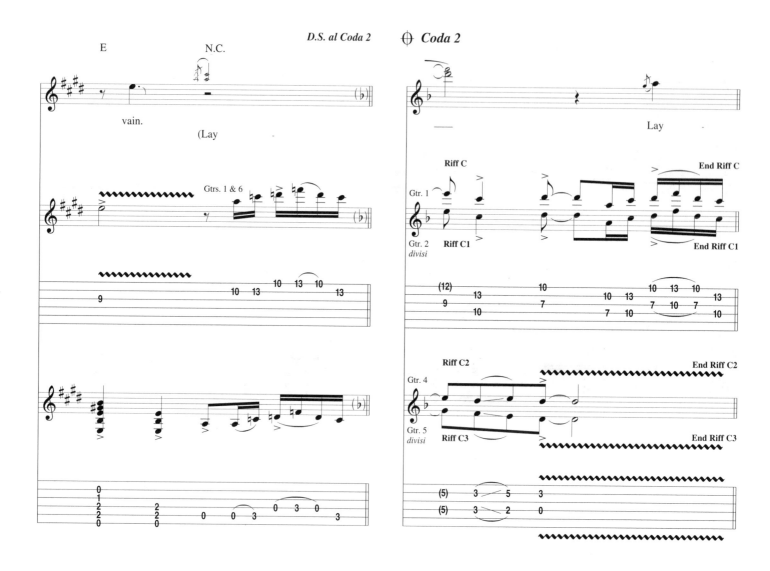

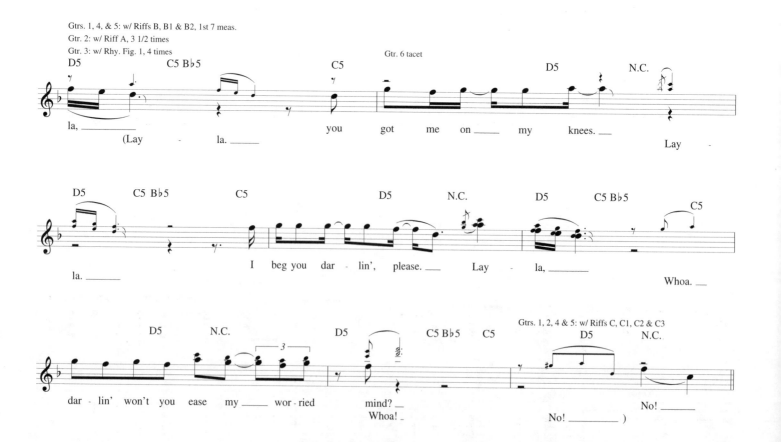

Guitar Solo

Gtrs. 1, 4, & 5: w/ Riffs B, B1 & B2, 1st 7 meas.
Gtr. 2: w/ Riff A, 3 1/2 times
Gtr. 3: w/ Rhy. Fig. 1, 11 1/2 times, simile

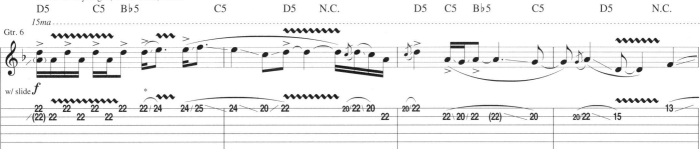

* TAB numbers based on location of notes beyond fretboard.

Gtrs. 1, 2,4 & 5: w/ Riffs C, C1, C2 & C3

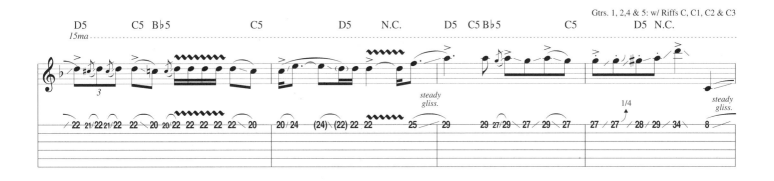

Gtrs. 1, 4 & 5: w/ Riffs B, B1 & B2, 1st 7 meas.
Gtr. 2: w/ Riff A, 3 1/2 times

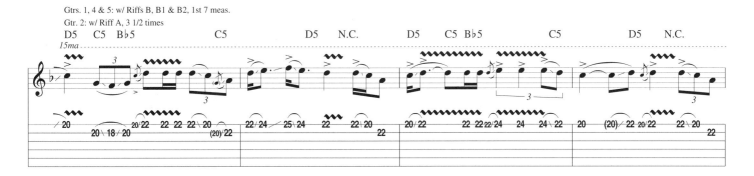

Gtrs. 1, 2, 4 & 5: w/ Riffs C, C1, C2, & C3

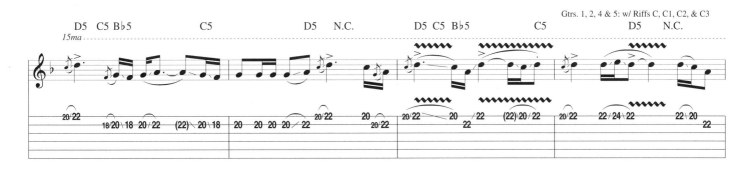

Gtrs. 1, 4 & 5: w/ Riffs B, B1 & B2, 1st 7 meas.
Gtr. 2: w/ Riff A, 3 1/2 times

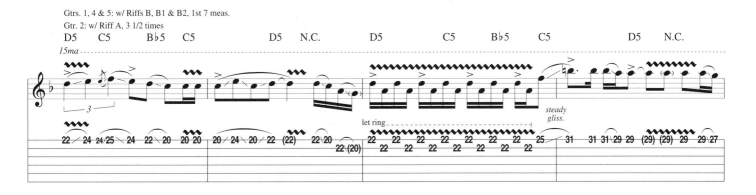

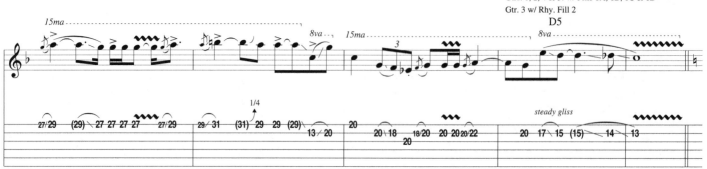

Interlude

All gtrs. tacet

Outro

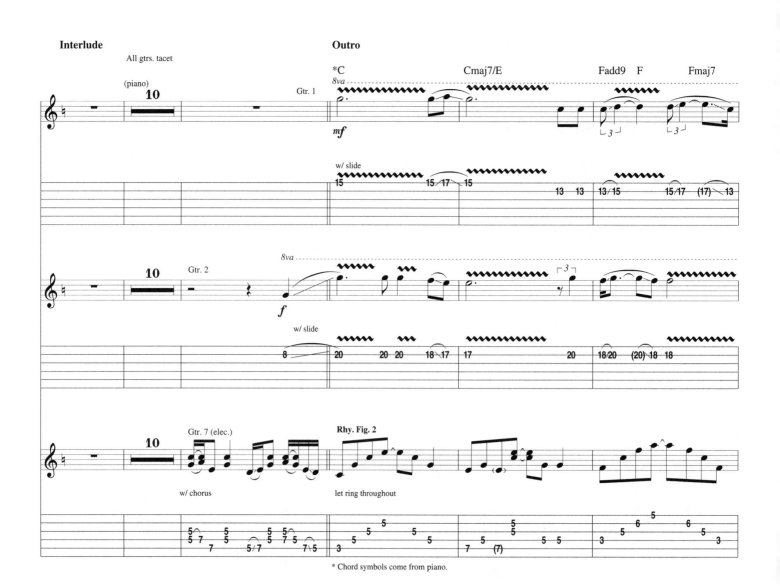

* Chord symbols come from piano.

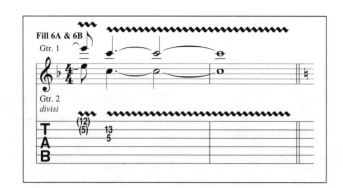

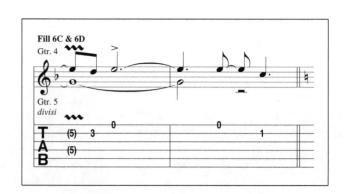

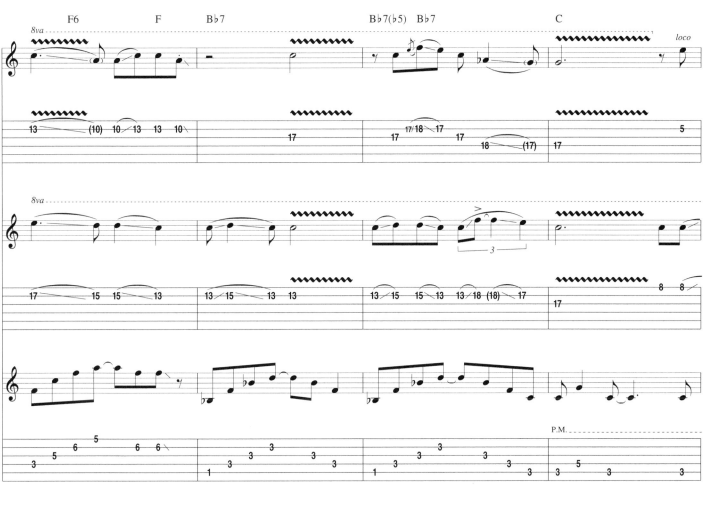

Gtr. 7: w/ Rhy. Fig. 2, 1st 5 meas., simile

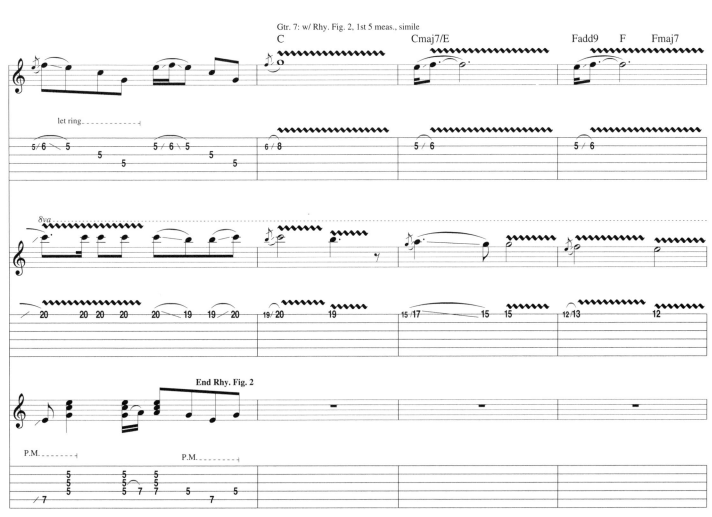

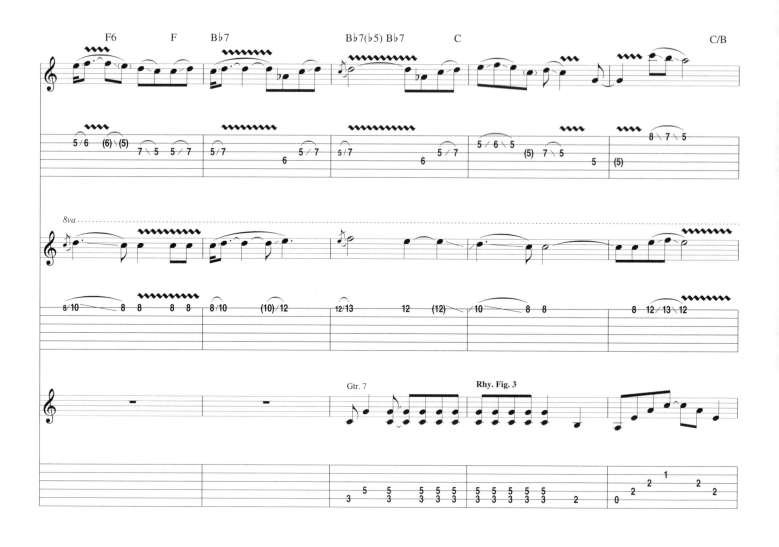

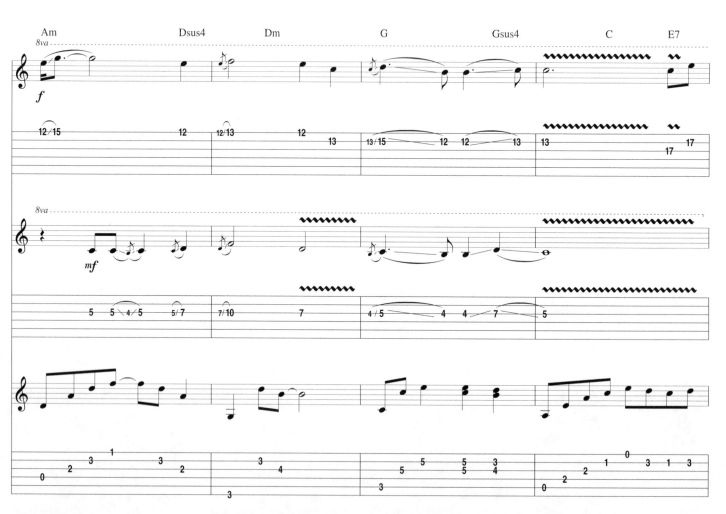

98

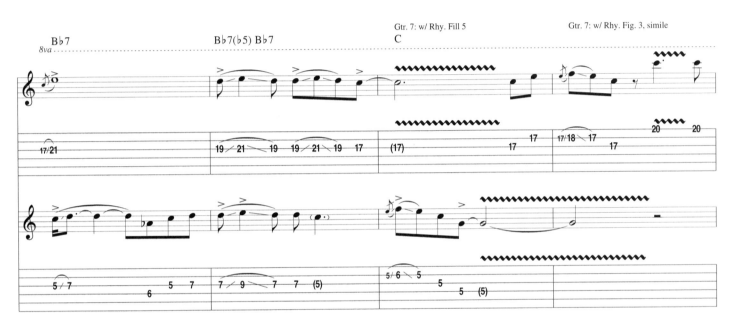

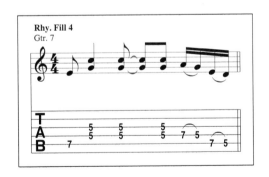

Gtr. 7: w/ Rhy. Fig. 2, simile
Gtr. 8: w/ Rhy. Fig. 4

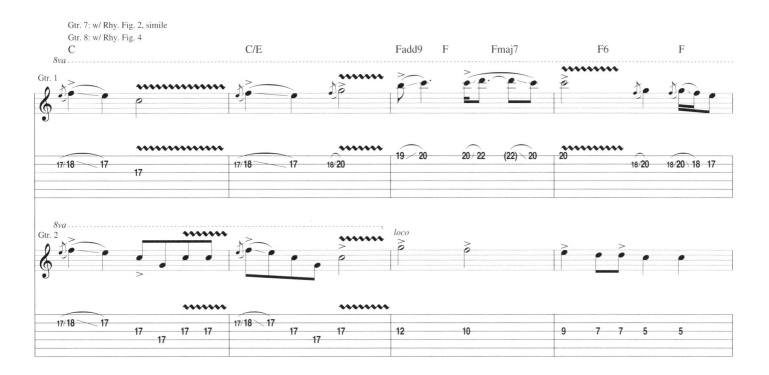

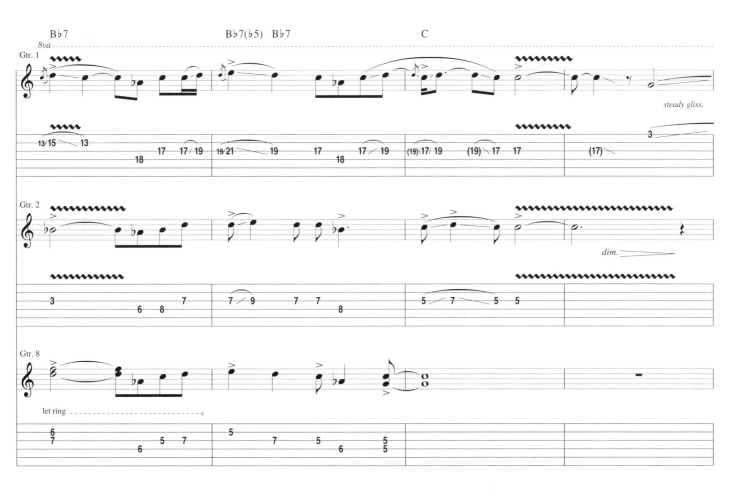

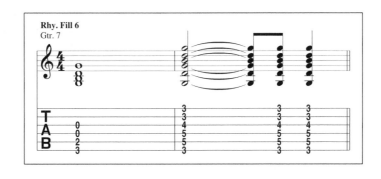

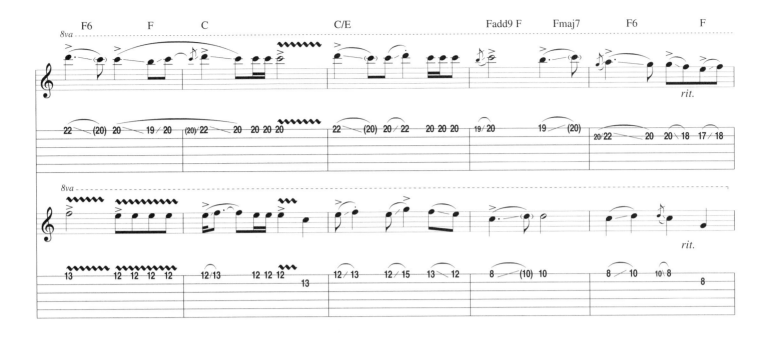

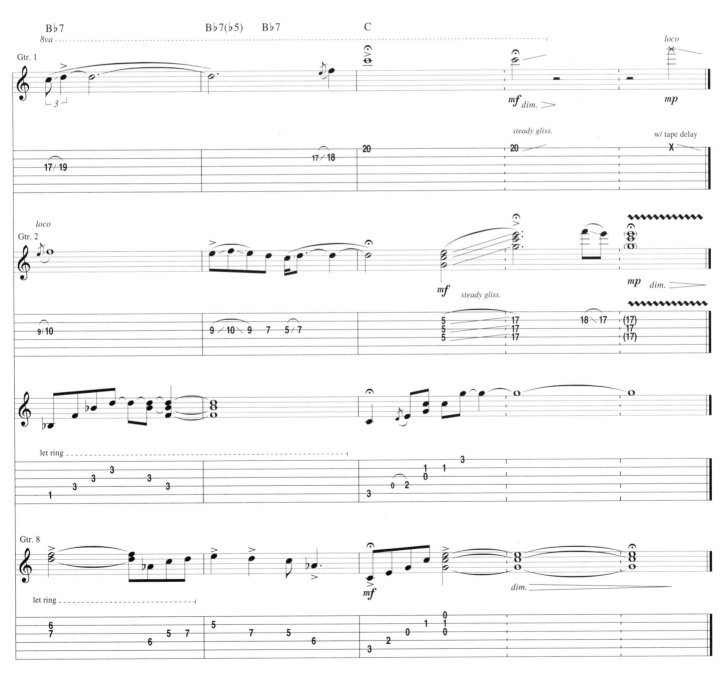

Let It Ride

Words and Music by Randy Bachman and Charles Turner

⊕ *Coda*

Interlude

Gtrs. 1, 2 & 3: w/ Rhy. Fig. 2, 2 times

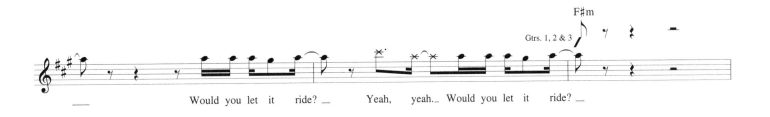

Would you let it ride? ___ Would you let it ride? _

___ Would you let it ride? _ Yeah, yeah._ Would you let it ride? _

Gtrs. 1, 2 & 3 tacet

Try, try, try to let it ride. ___

Try, try, try to let it ride. ___ Yeah, yeah, yeah. Try, try, try to let it ride._

Oh, ___ oh. Try, try, try to let it ride._

Try, try, try to let it ride. _____ Would you let it ride?

(sing on last repeat)

Would you let it ride? _____ Would you let it ride? _____

_____ Would you let it ride? _____

Outro

Fade Out

Long Cool Woman (In a Black Dress)

Words and Music by Allan Clarke, Roger Cook and Roger Greenaway

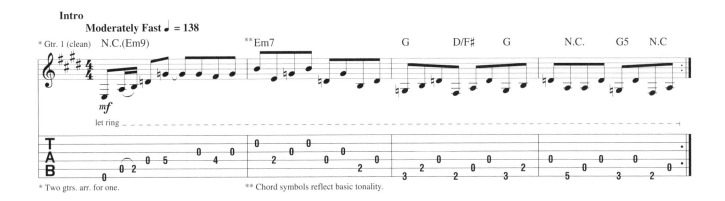

* Two gtrs. arr. for one. ** Chord symbols reflect basic tonality.

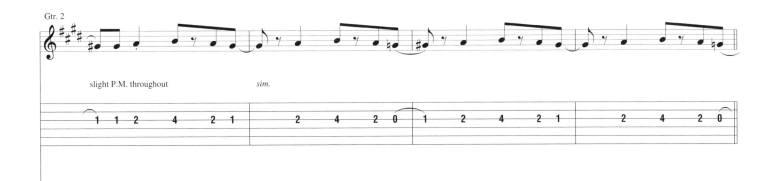

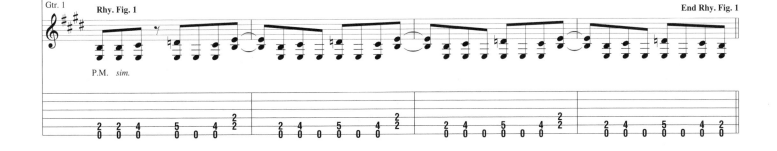

Verse

1. Sat-ur-day night _ I was down-town,   work - in' for the F. B. I. _

_ _ _ Sit - tin' in a nest   of bad   men, _   whis -

Gtr. 2: w/ Rhy. Fig. 3, 3 times, simile

Char - lie said," I hope that you're a - ble boy. 'cause I'm tell - in' you she knows _ where it's at." _

Gtr. 1: w/ Rhy. Fig. 2, simile

Well, sud - den - ly we heard the si - rens, and

ev - 'ry - bod - y start - ed to run. _____ A jump - in' out of doors and ta -

- bles, well, I heard ___ some - bod - y shoot - in' a gun. _____

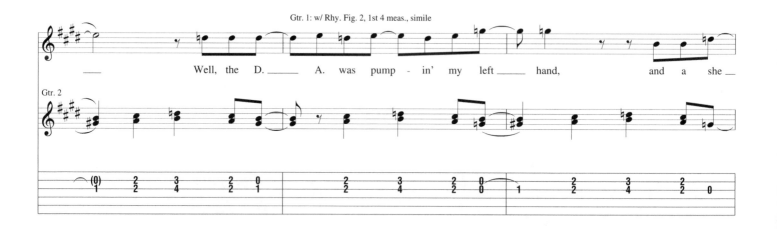

Gtr. 1: w/ Rhy. Fig. 2, 1st 4 meas., simile

Well, the D. ___ A. was pump - in' my left ___ hand, and a she ___

Gtr. 2

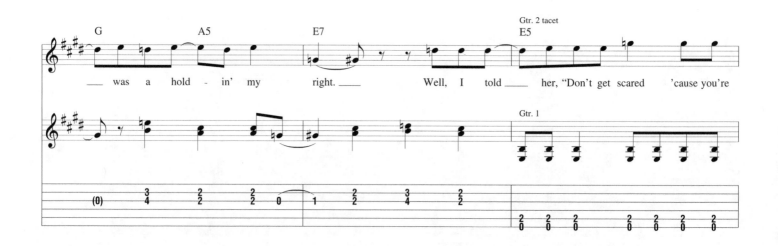

___ was a hold - in' my right. ___ Well, I told ___ her, "Don't get scared 'cause you're

gon - na be spared." Well, I got-ta be _____ for - giv - en if I'm wan-na spend my liv - in' with a

 Coda

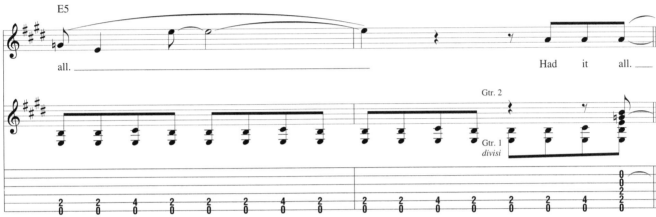

all. _____ Had it all. _____

Outro

Gtr. 1: w/ Rhy. Fig. 1, simile, till fade
Gtr. 2: w/ Rhy. Fig. 3, 1st 2 meas., simile, till fade

_____ Had it all. _____ Had it all!

Had it all! Had it all!

Begin Fade

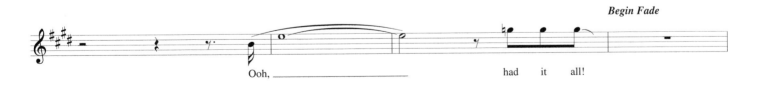

Ooh, _____ had it all!

Fade Out

Ah, she had it all. Yeah.

Mississippi Queen

Words and Music by Leslie West, Felix Pappalardi, Corky Laing and David Rea

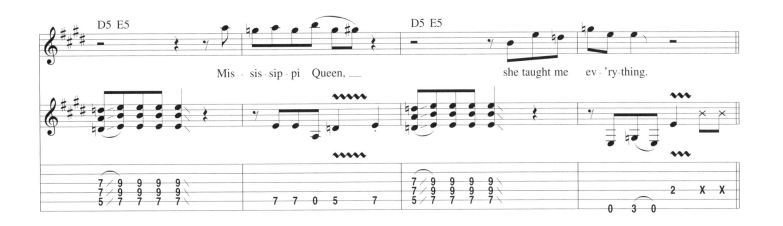

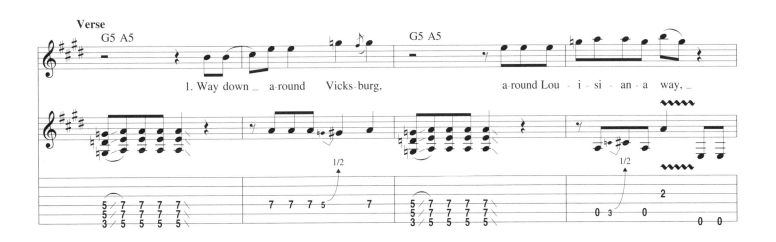

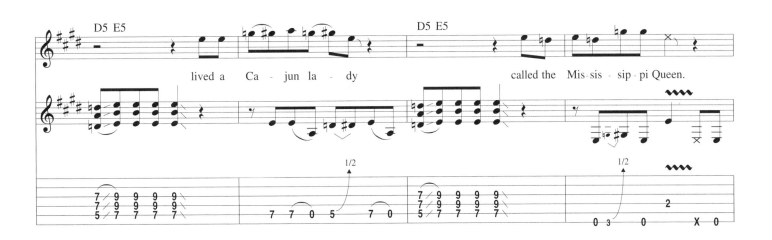

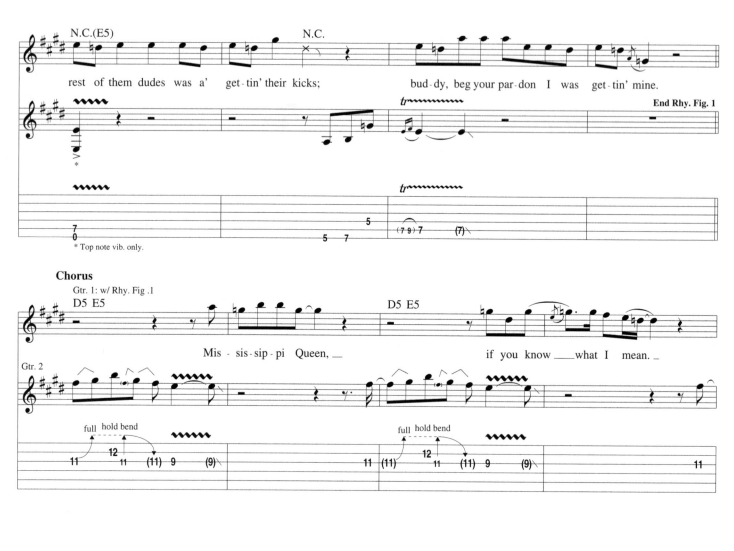

rest of them dudes was a' get-tin' their kicks; bud-dy, beg your par-don I was get-tin' mine.

End Rhy. Fig. 1

* Top note vib. only.

Chorus

Gtr. 1: w/ Rhy. Fig .1

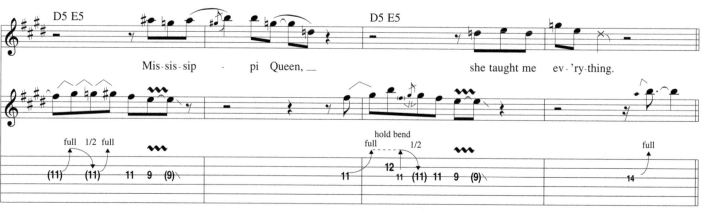

Mis-sis-sip-pi Queen, __ if you know __ what I mean. __

Gtr. 2

Mis-sis-sip - pi Queen, __ she taught me ev-'ry-thing.

Verse

2. This la - dy she __ asked me if I would be her man. __

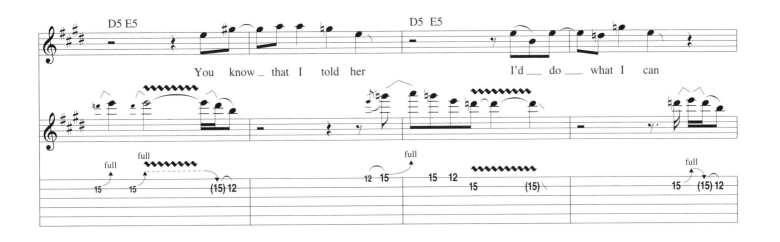

You know ___ that I told her I'd ___ do ___ what I can

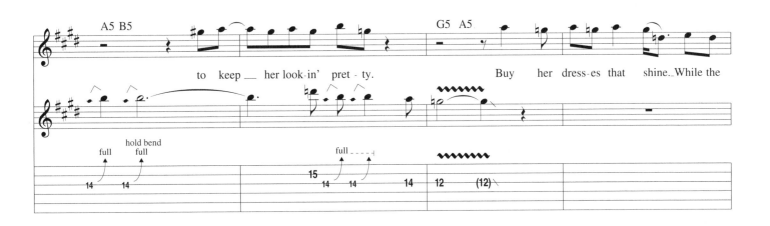

to keep ___ her look-in' pret-ty. Buy her dress-es that shine. While the

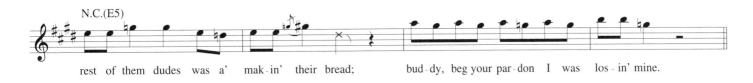

rest of them dudes was a' mak-in' their bread; bud-dy, beg your par-don I was los-in' mine.

Guitar Solo

Gtr. 1: w/ Rhy. Fig. 1, 1st 23 meas. only

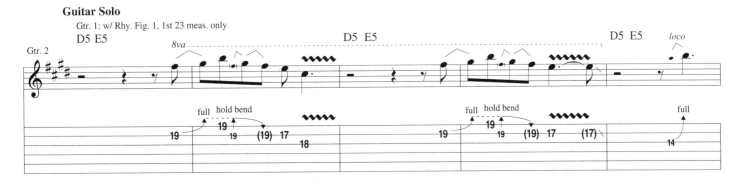

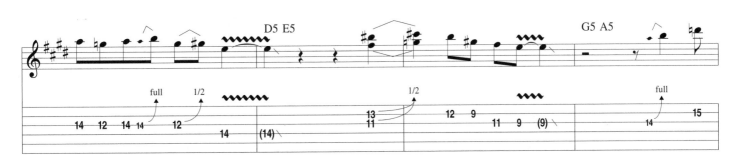

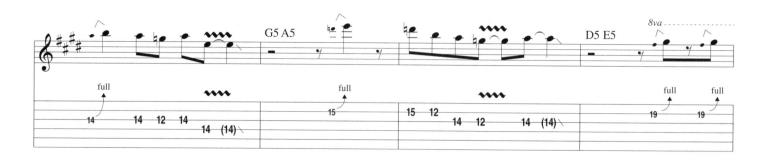

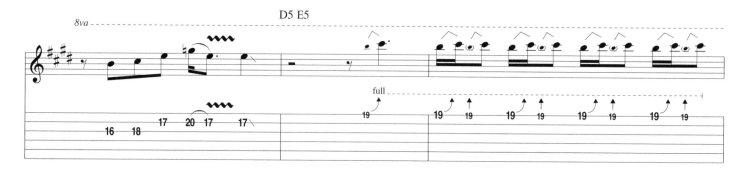

You know __ she was a danc - er, ___ she moved __ bet - ter on wine. While the

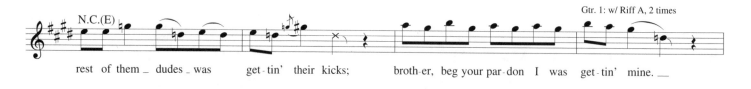

rest of them __ dudes __ was get - tin' their kicks; broth - er, beg your par - don I was get - tin' mine. __

Hey, _____ Mis - sis - sip - pi Queen. __

Ridin' the Storm Out

Words and Music by Gary Richrath

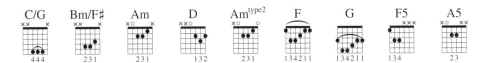

Intro
Moderately Fast Rock ♩ = 142

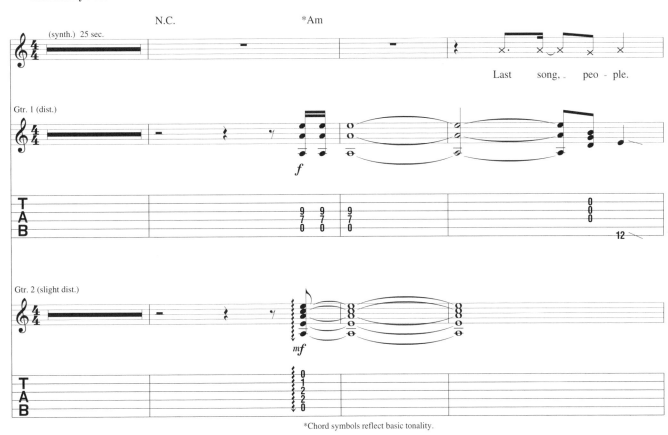

*Chord symbols reflect basic tonality.

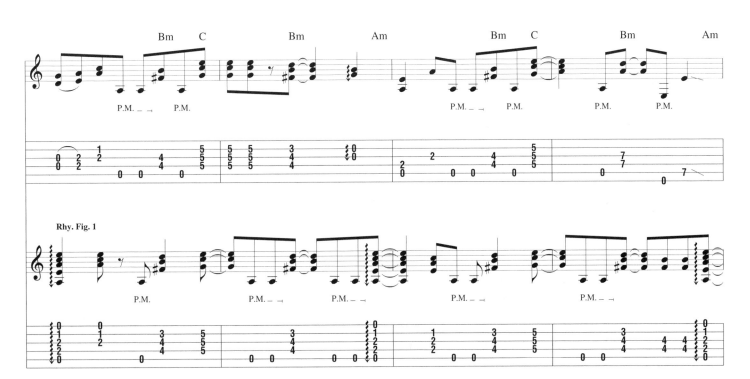

Verse

Gtr. 2: w/ Rhy. Fig. 1, 1 5/8 times, simile

2. La - dy be - side ___ me, well, she's a there to guide ___ me.

She says a that a - lone, ___ we've a fi - nal - ly found ___ our ___ home ___ Well, the wind ___

pitch: E E E E   E E E E

*applies to harmonics

___ out - side ___ is a fright - 'nin', ___ but it's kind - er than a light - nin' life ___ in the cit - y. A

pitch: E

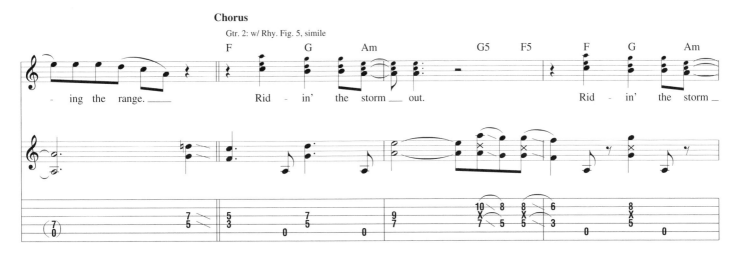

Chorus

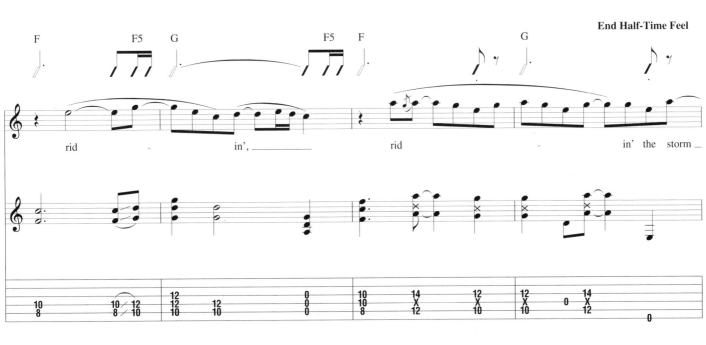

Smoke on the Water

Words and Music by Ritchie Blackmore, Ian Gillan,
Roger Glover, Jon Lord and Ian Paice

*Chord symbols reflect implied tonality.

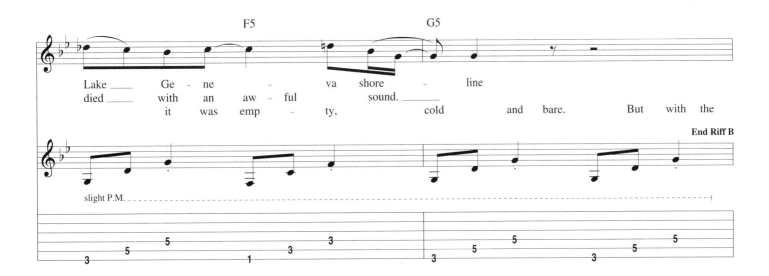

to make rec-ords with the mo-bile, _____ we did-n't
A Fun-ky Claude was run-ning in and out, pull-ing
Roll-ing truck Stones thing just out-side, mak-ing our

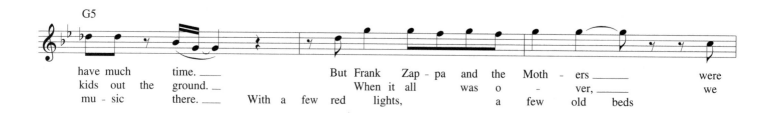

have much time. _____ But Frank Zap-pa and the Moth-ers _____ were
kids out the ground. _ When it all was o - ver, _____ we
mu-sic there. ____ With a few red lights, a few old beds

at the best place a - round. _____ But some stu-pid with a
had to find an-oth-er place. _____ But Swiss time was
we made a place to sweat. ____ No mat-ter what we

flare gun burned the place to the _____ ground. ____
run-ning out; it seemed that we would lose the race. _____
get out of this, I know, I know we'll nev-er for-get.

Chorus

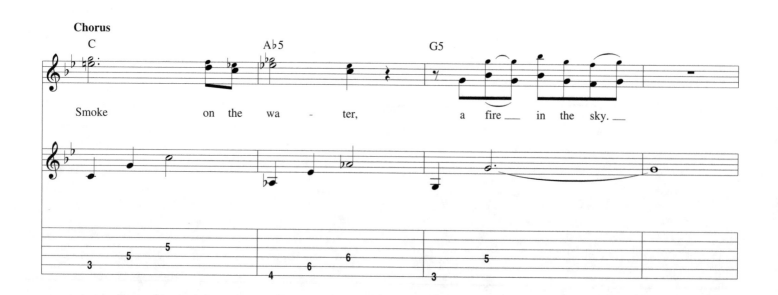

Smoke on the wa - ter, a fire ___ in the sky. ___

134

⊕ Coda

Outro-Organ Solo

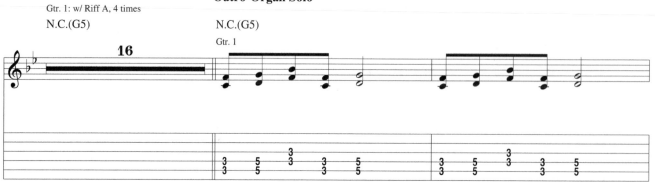

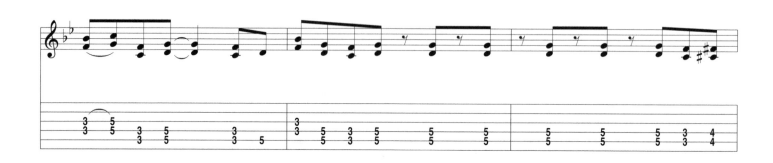

Susie - Q

Words and Music by Dale Hawkins, Stan Lewis and Eleanor Broadwater

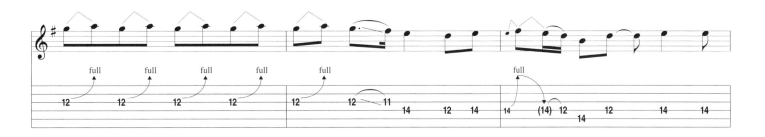

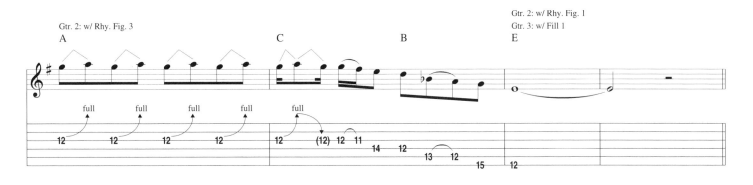

Gtr. 2: w/ Rhy. Fig. 3

Gtr. 2: w/ Rhy. Fig. 1
Gtr. 3: w/ Fill 1

1., 2., 3.　　　　　　*4.*

D.S. al Coda 1

Interlude

Gtr. 2: w/ Rhy. Fig. 1

Em7

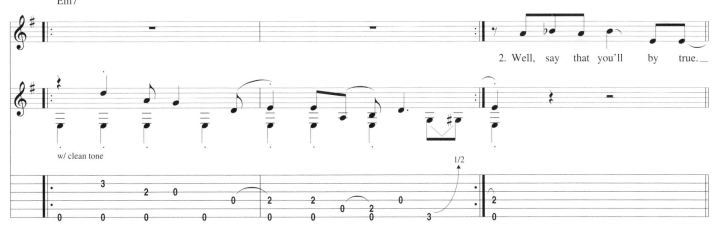

2. Well, say that you'll by true.___

w/ clean tone

⊕ *Coda 1*

Guitar Solo

Gtr. 2: w/ Rhy. Fig. 1, 4 times

E

Gtr. 1

let ring

let ring

Fill 1

Gtr. 3

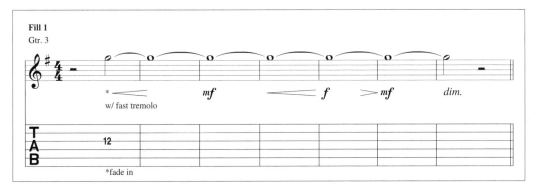

w/ fast tremolo

*fade in

⊕ Coda 2

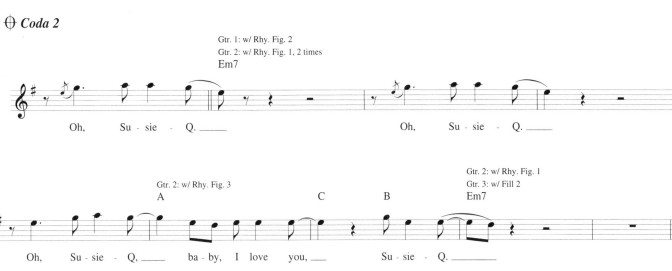

Oh, Su - sie - Q. ___ Oh, Su - sie - Q. ___

Oh, Su - sie - Q, ___ ba - by, I love you, ___ Su - sie - Q. ___

Outro-Solo

Gtr. 2: w/ Rhy. Fig. 1, till fade, simile

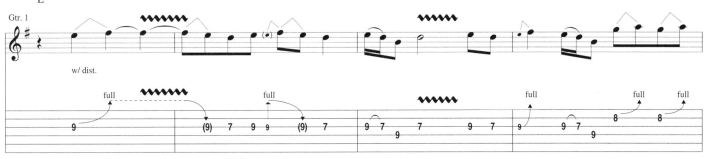

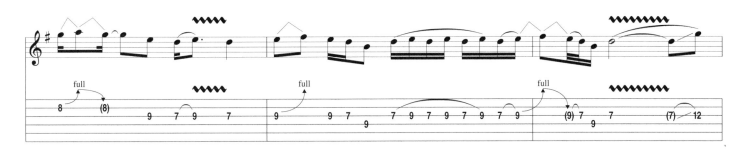

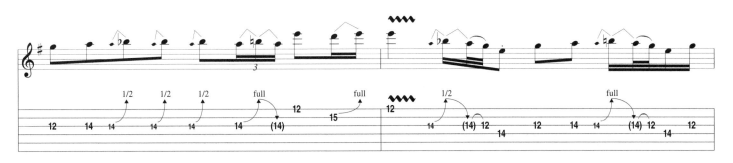

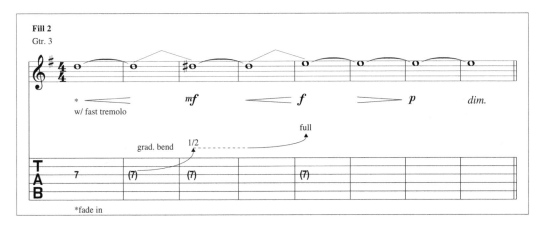

143

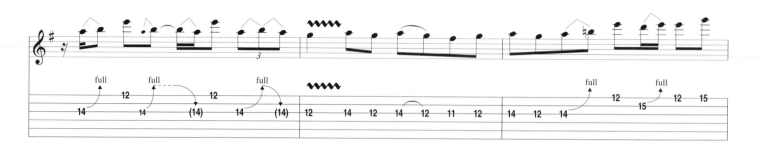

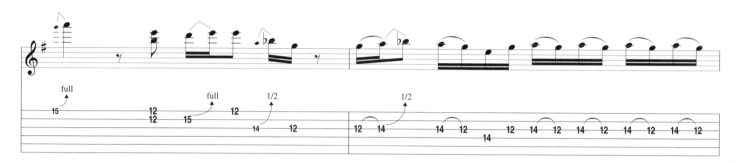

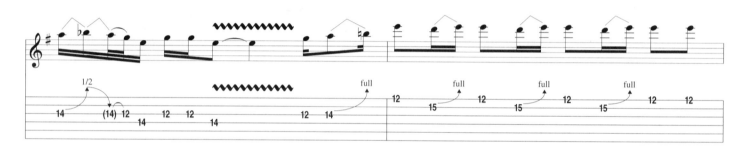

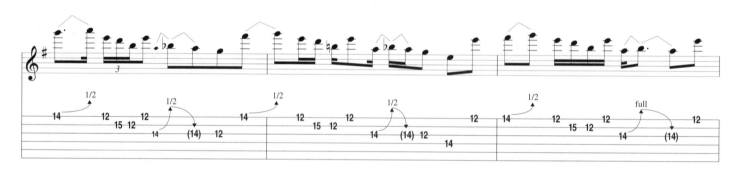

Begin Fade

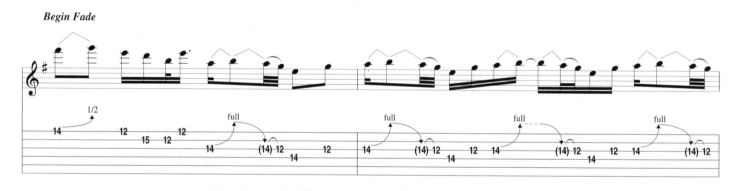

Fade Out

144

Sweet Emotion

Words and Music by Steven Tyler and Tom Hamilton

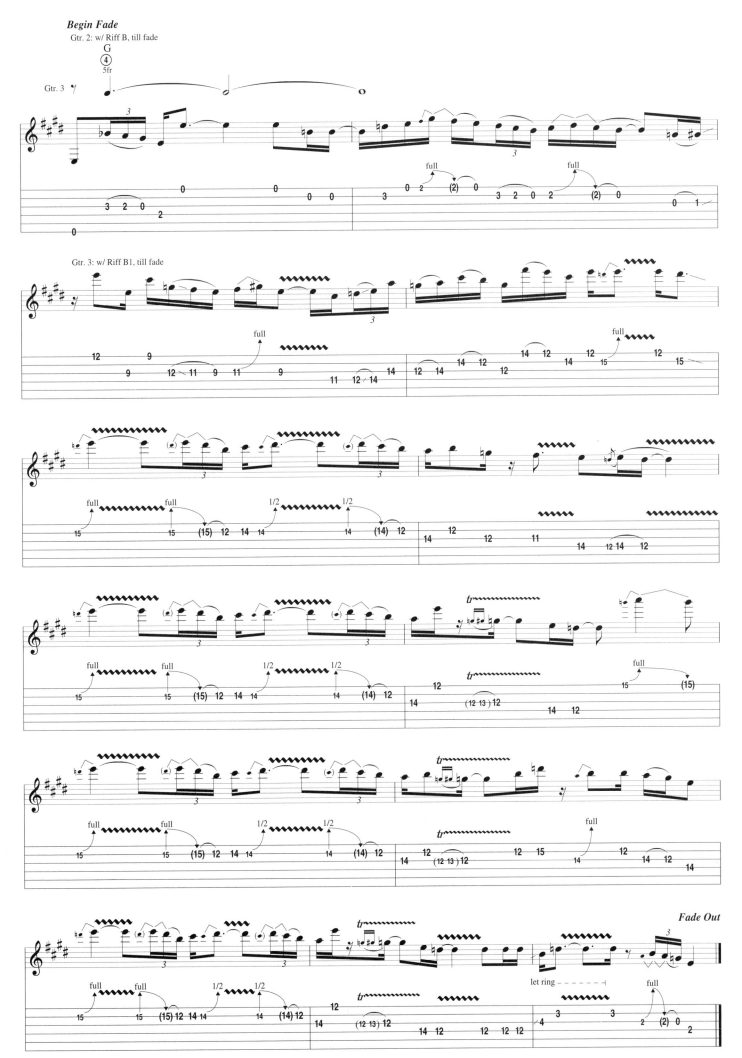

White Room

Words and Music by Jack Bruce and Pete Brown

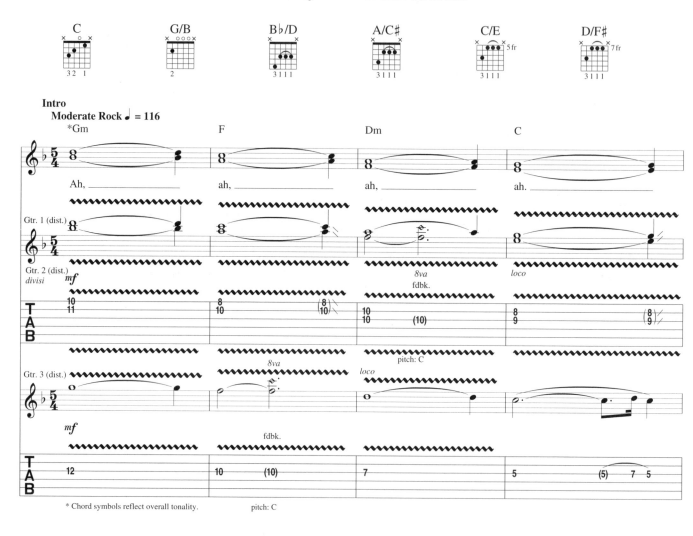

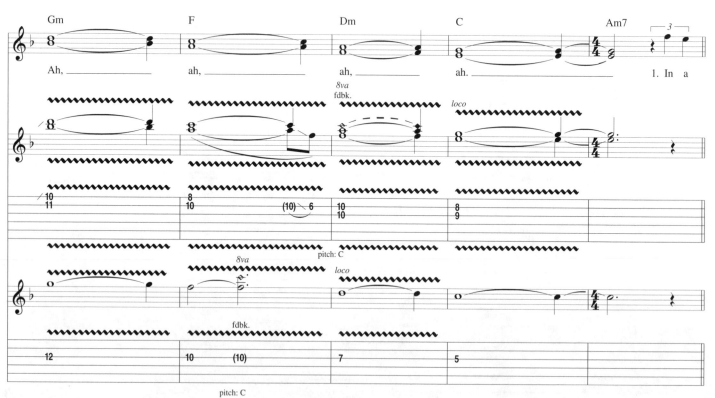

Verse

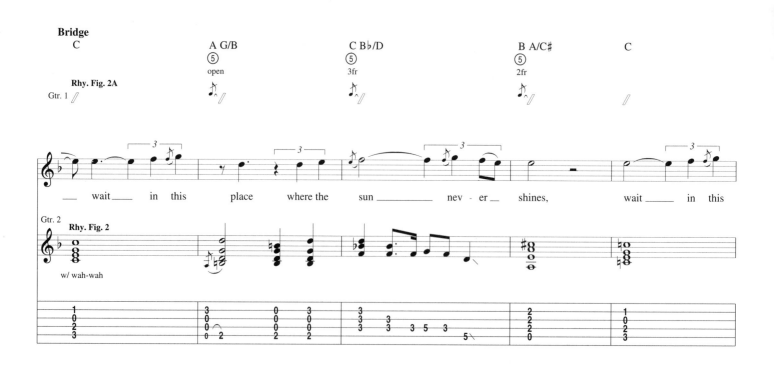

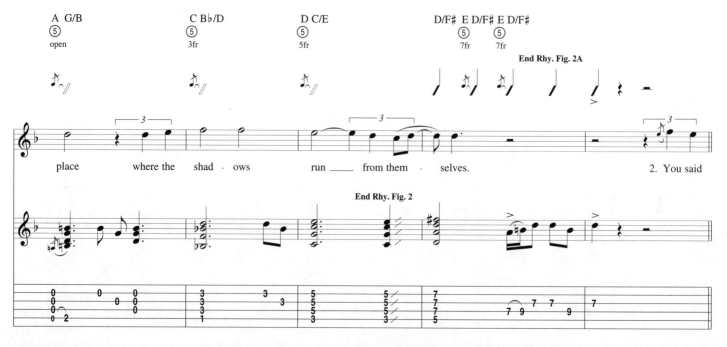

Verse

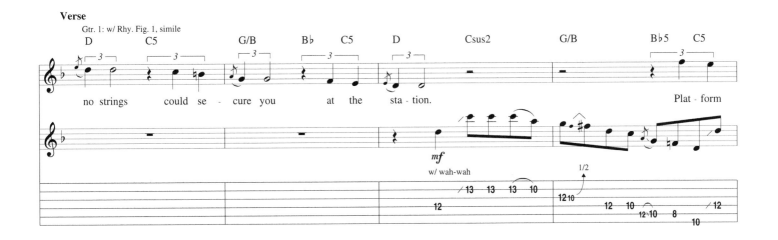

no strings could se - cure you at the sta - tion. Plat - form

tick - et, rest - less die - sel, good - bye win - dows. I walked

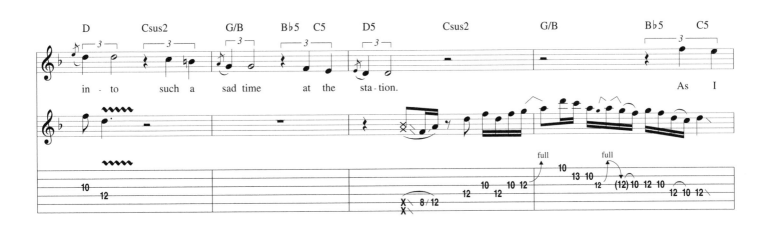

in - to such a sad time at the sta - tion. As I

walked out _ felt my own need just be - gin - ning. I'll _

Bridge

wait _____ in the queue when the trains _____ come _____ back.

Lie _____ with _____ you where the shad - ows run _____ from them - selves. _____

Interlude

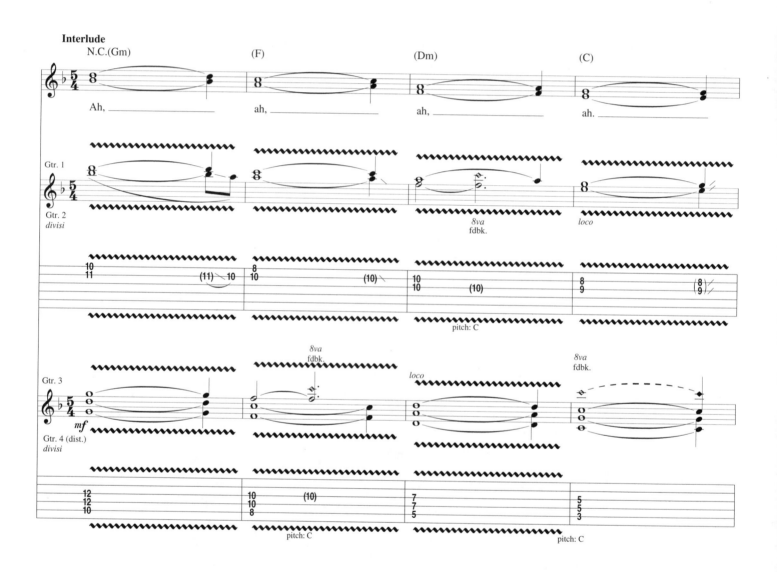

156

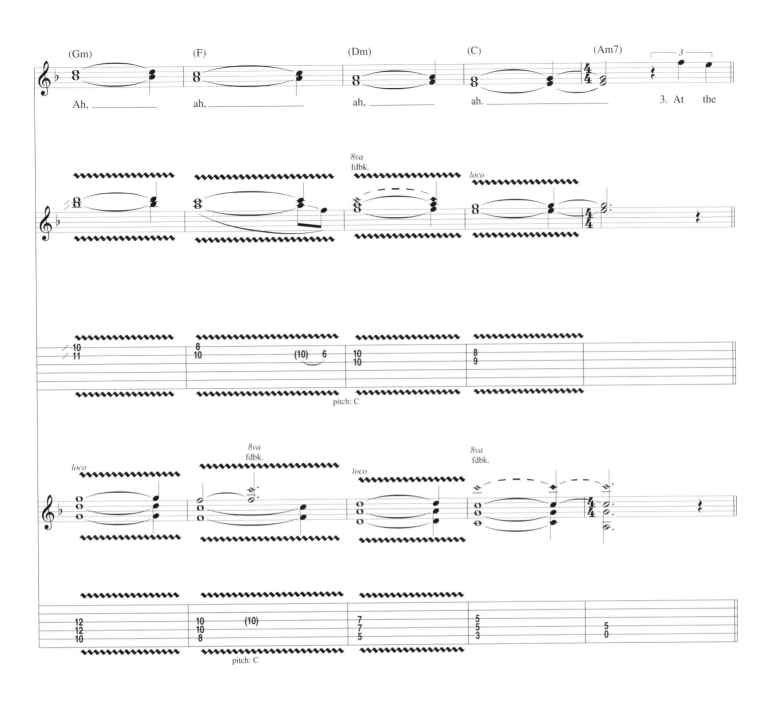

Ah, _____ ah, _____ ah, _____ ah. 3. At the

Verse

Gtrs. 3 & 4 tacet
Gtr. 1: w/ Rhy. Fig. 1, simile

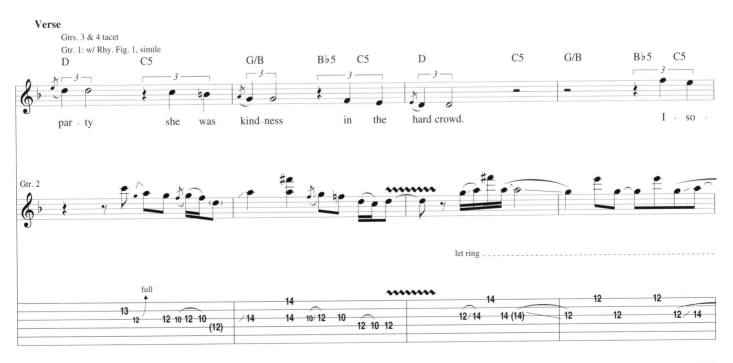

par - ty she was kind-ness in the hard crowd. I - so -

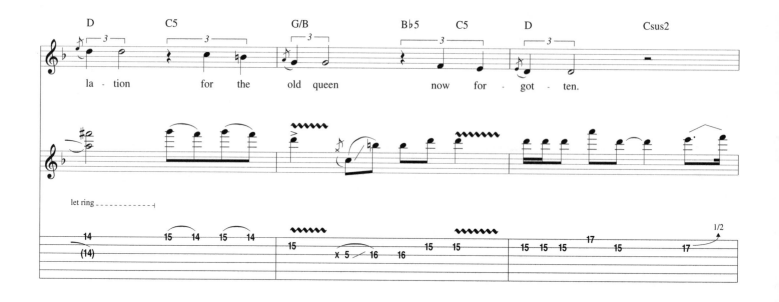

la - tion   for the   old queen   now for - got - ten.

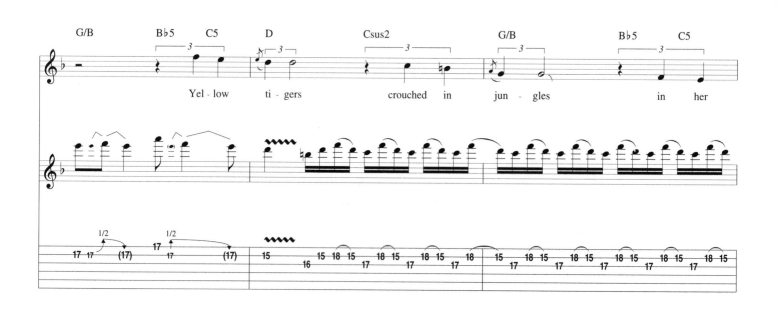

Yel - low   ti - gers   crouched in   jun - gles   in her

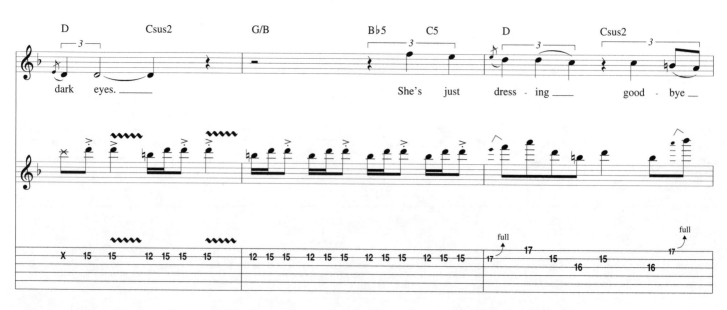

dark   eyes.   She's just   dress - ing   good - bye

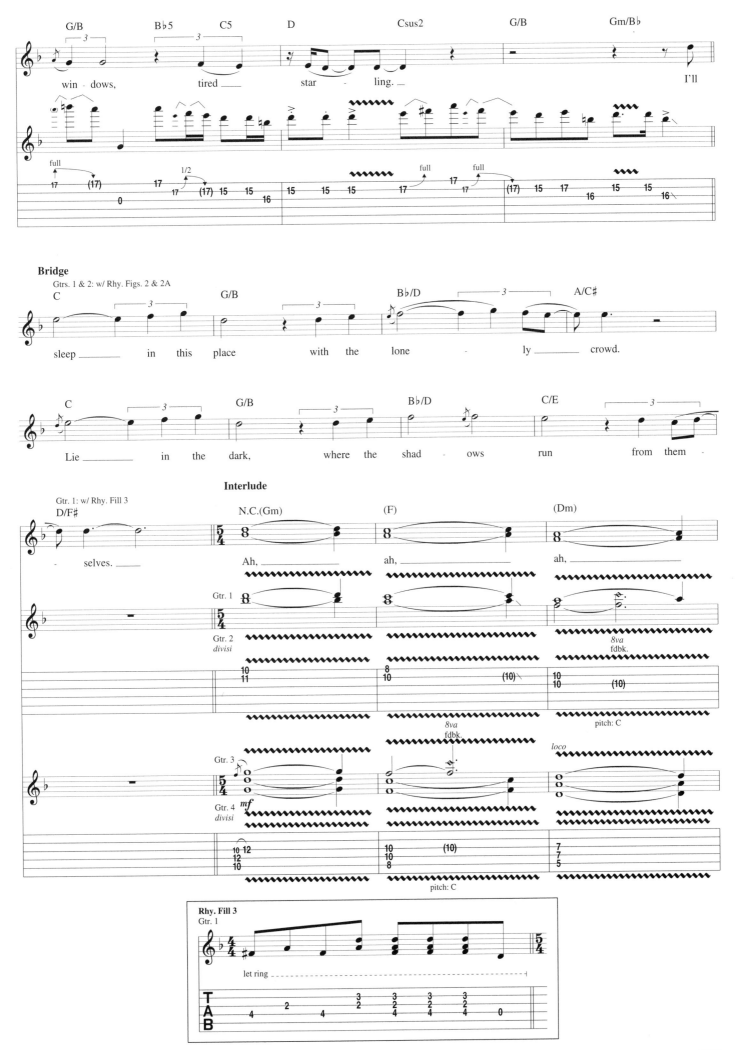

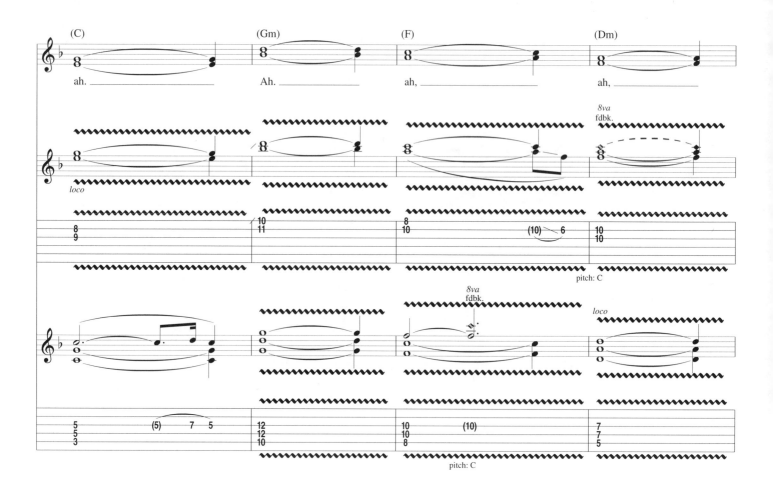

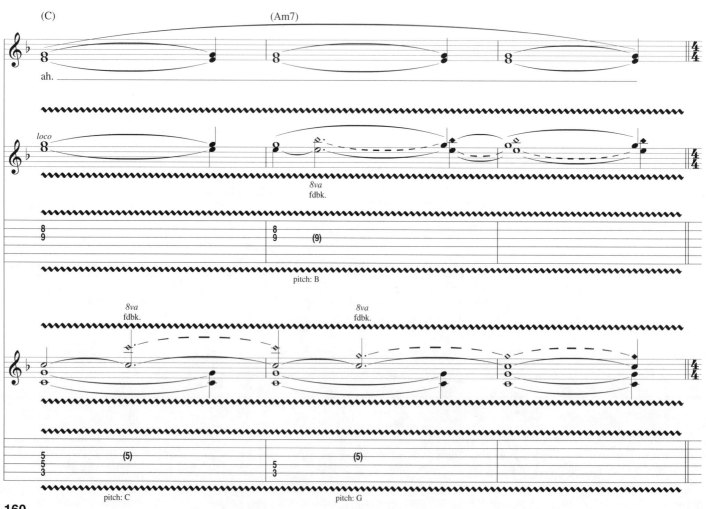

Outro-Guitar Solo

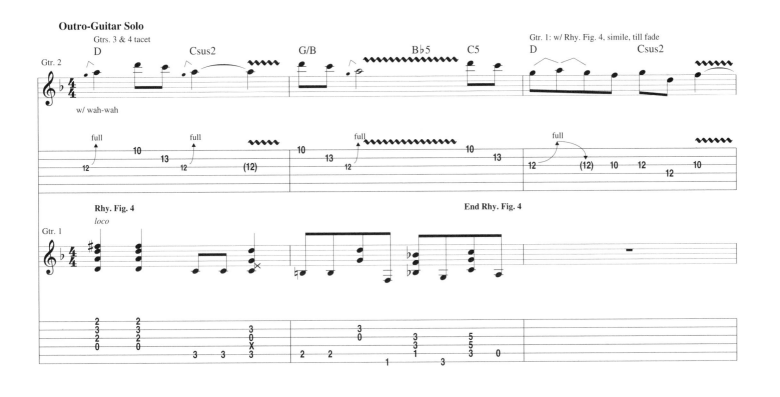

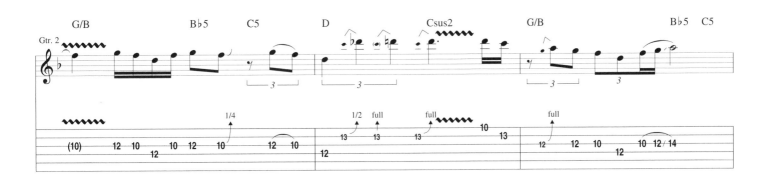

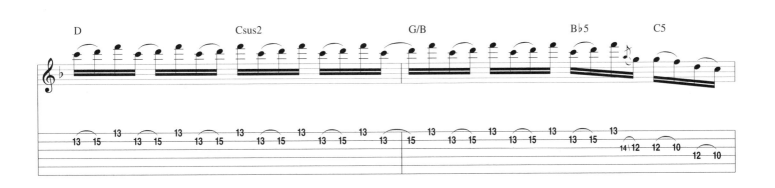

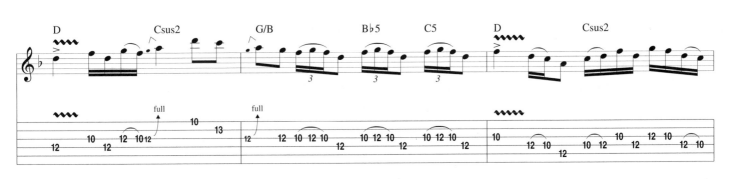

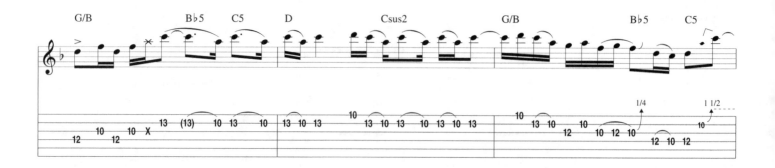

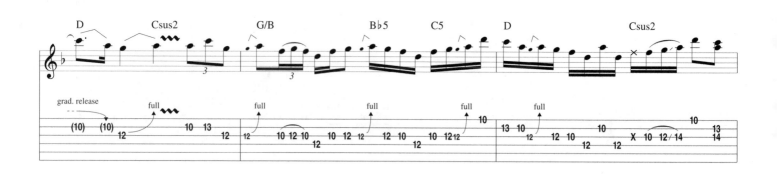

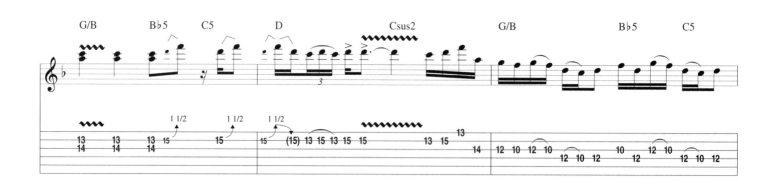

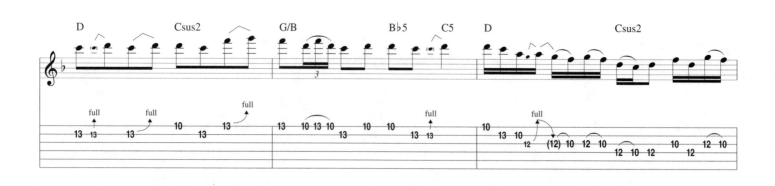

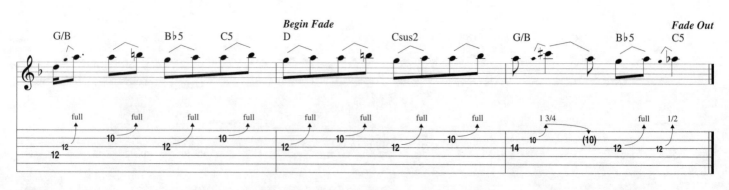

With a Little Help From My Friends

Words and Music by John Lennon and Paul McCartney

sad   'cause you're   on   your ___ own?)   I   tell ya don't ___ e - ven   say   it   no   more.

Chorus

Gon - na   get   by   with   my   friends,

yeah.   Yeah, ___ yeah, ___ yeah,   I'm gon - na

try.   Keep   on   get - tin'   high - er   with 'em.

* played as even eighth notes

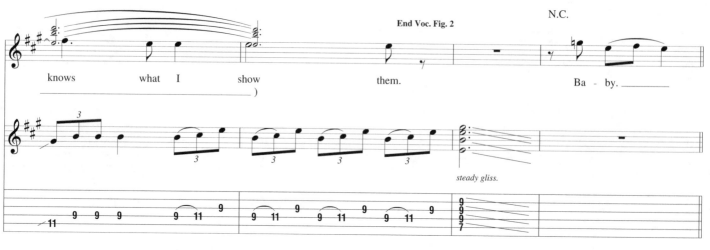

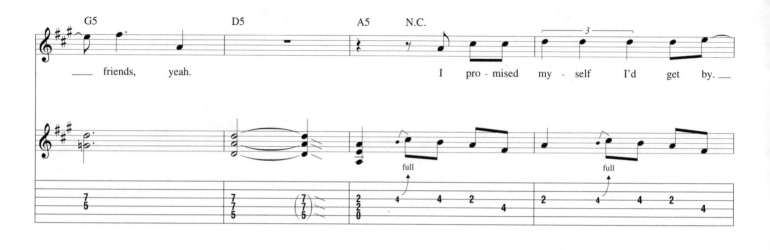

friends, yeah.

_I pro-mised my-self I'd get by. _

_Said, I'm gon-na try it with 'em, _ too, huh. _

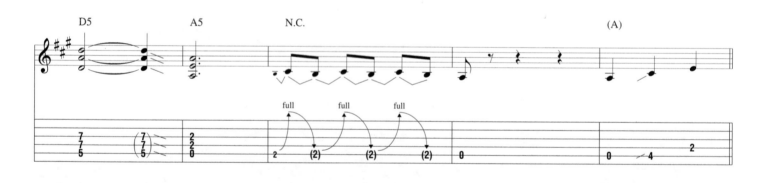

Bridge

(Do you need an - y - bod - y?)

_Whoa, _

steady gliss.

Outro-Chorus

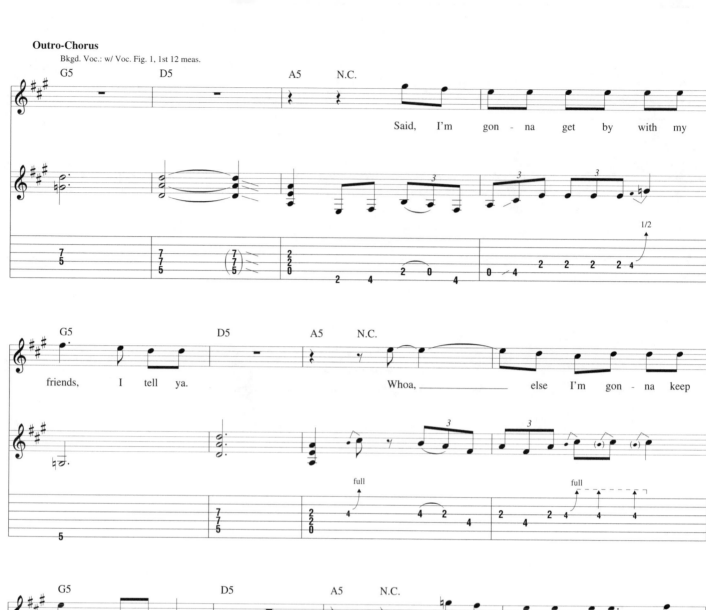

You Shook Me

Written by Willie Dixon and J.B. Lenoir

me ba - by, ___ you shook me all ___ night long. _____

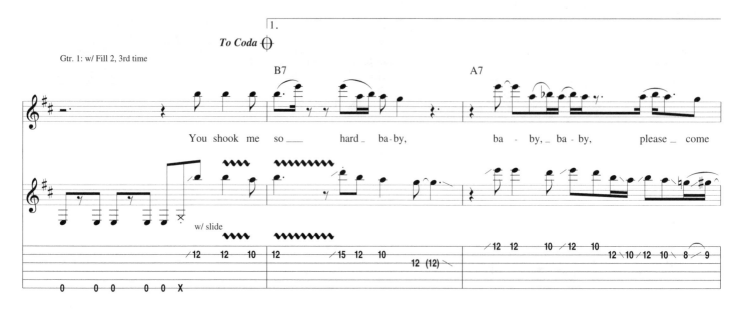

To Coda ⊕

Gtr. 1: w/ Fill 2, 3rd time

You shook me so ___ hard _ ba-by, ba - by, _ ba - by, please _ come

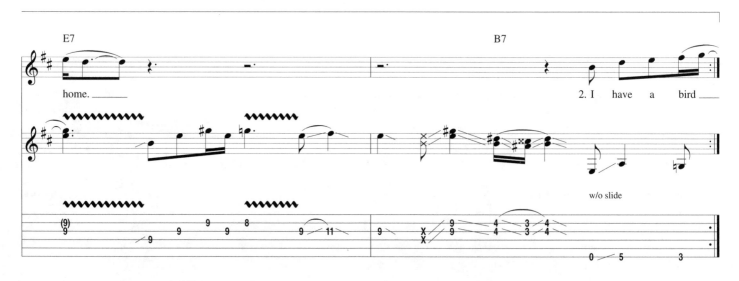

home. _____ 2. I have a bird ___

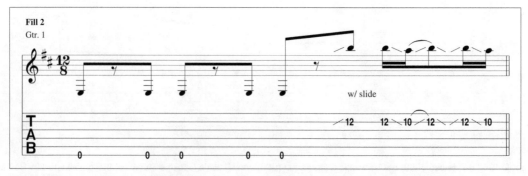

Fill 2
Gtr. 1

180

3. You _ know you

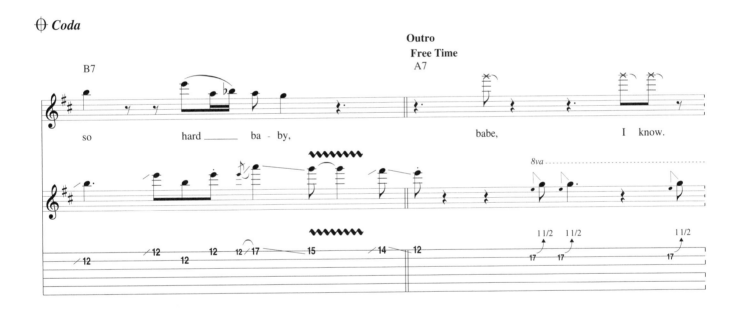

so   hard _____ ba - by,   babe,   I know.

Oh, oh!   Oh, oh! _   Oh, oh, oh! _

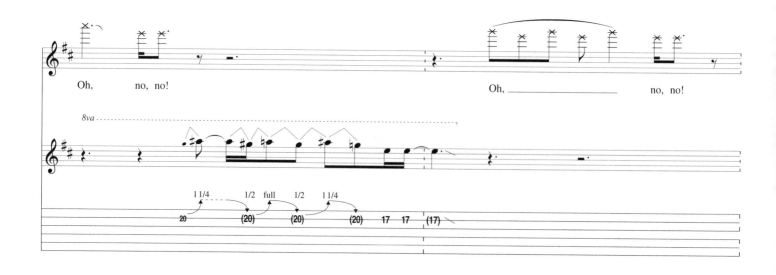

Oh,   no, no!   Oh, _____   no, no!

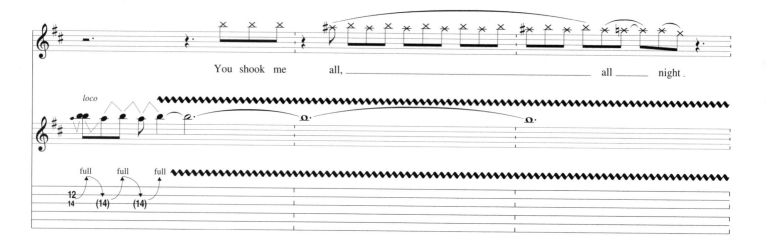

You shook me   all, _____   all ____ night .

long. _____   A5   E

Additional Lyrics

2. I have a bird that whistles and
   I have birds that sing.
   I have a bird that whistles and
   I have birds that sing.
   I have a bird won't do nothin; oh, oh, oh, oh,
   without a diamond ring.

3. You know you shook me, babe,
   You shook me all night long.
   I know you really, really did, babe.
   I think you shook me, baby,
   You shook me all night long.
   You shook me so hard, baby, I know.

Guitar Notation Legend

Guitar Music can be notated three different ways: on a *musical staff*, in *tablature*, and in *rhythm slashes*.

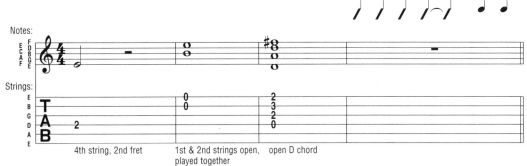

RHYTHM SLASHES are written above the staff. Strum chords in the rhythm indicated. Use the chord diagrams found at the top of the first page of the transcription for the appropriate chord voicings. Round noteheads indicate single notes.

THE MUSICAL STAFF shows pitches and rhythms and is divided by bar lines into measures. Pitches are named after the first seven letters of the alphabet.

TABLATURE graphically represents the guitar fingerboard. Each horizontal line represents a string, and each number represents a fret.

4th string, 2nd fret   1st & 2nd strings open,   open D chord
played together

HALF-STEP BEND: Strike the note and bend up 1/2 step.

BEND AND RELEASE: Strike the note and bend up as indicated, then release back to the original note. Only the first note is struck.

HAMMER-ON: Strike the first (lower) note with one finger, then sound the higher note (on the same string) with another finger by fretting it without picking.

TRILL: Very rapidly alternate between the notes indicated by continuously hammering on and pulling off.

PICK SCRAPE: The edge of the pick is rubbed down (or up) the string, producing a scratchy sound.

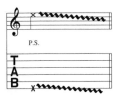

TREMOLO PICKING: The note is picked as rapidly and continuously as possible.

WHOLE-STEP BEND: Strike the note and bend up one step.

PRE-BEND: Bend the note as indicated, then strike it.

PULL-OFF: Place both fingers on the notes to be sounded. Strike the first note and without picking, pull the finger off to sound the second (lower) note.

TAPPING: Hammer ("tap") the fret indicated with the pick-hand index or middle finger and pull off to the note fretted by the fret hand.

MUFFLED STRINGS: A percussive sound is produced by laying the fret hand across the string(s) without depressing, and striking them with the pick hand.

VIBRATO BAR DIVE AND RETURN: The pitch of the note or chord is dropped a specified number of steps (in rhythm) then returned to the original pitch.

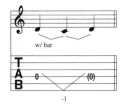

GRACE NOTE BEND: Strike the note and bend up as indicated. The first note does not take up any time.

VIBRATO: The string is vibrated by rapidly bending and releasing the note with the fretting hand.

LEGATO SLIDE: Strike the first note and then slide the same fret-hand finger up or down to the second note. The second note is not struck.

NATURAL HARMONIC: Strike the note while the fret-hand lightly touches the string directly over the fret indicated.

PALM MUTING: The note is partially muted by the pick hand lightly touching the string(s) just before the bridge.

VIBRATO BAR SCOOP: Depress the bar just before striking the note, then quickly release the bar.

SLIGHT (MICROTONE) BEND: Strike the note and bend up 1/4 step.

WIDE VIBRATO: The pitch is varied to a greater degree by vibrating with the fretting hand.

SHIFT SLIDE: Same as legato slide, except the second note is struck.

PINCH HARMONIC: The note is fretted normally and a harmonic is produced by adding the edge of the thumb or the tip of the index finger of the pick hand to the normal pick attack.

RAKE: Drag the pick across the strings indicated with a single motion.

VIBRATO BAR DIP: Strike the note and then immediately drop a specified number of steps, then release back to the original pitch.

RECORDED VERSIONS
The Best Note-For-Note Transcriptions Available

ALL BOOKS INCLUDE TABLATURE

00690016 Will Ackerman Collection $19.95
00690199 Aerosmith – Nine Lives $19.95
00690146 Aerosmith – Toys in the Attic $19.95
00694865 Alice In Chains – Dirt $19.95
00694932 Allman Brothers Band – Volume 1 . . . . $24.95
00694933 Allman Brothers Band – Volume 2 . . . . $24.95
00694934 Allman Brothers Band – Volume 3 . . . . $24.95
00694877 Chet Atkins – Guitars For All Seasons . . $19.95
00694918 Randy Bachman Collection $22.95
00694880 Beatles – Abbey Road $19.95
00694863 Beatles –
　　　　　Sgt. Pepper's Lonely Hearts Club Band . $19.95
00690383 Beatles – Yellow Submarine $19.95
00690174 Beck – Mellow Gold $17.95
00690346 Beck – Mutations $19.95
00690175 Beck – Odelay $17.95
00694884 The Best of George Benson $19.95
00692385 Chuck Berry $19.95
00692200 Black Sabbath –
　　　　　We Sold Our Soul For Rock 'N' Roll . . $19.95
00690115 Blind Melon – Soup $19.95
00690305 Blink 182 – Dude Ranch $19.95
00690028 Blue Oyster Cult – Cult Classics $19.95
00690219 Blur $19.95
00694935 Boston: Double Shot Of $22.95
00690237 Meredith Brooks – Blurring the Edges . . $19.95
00690168 Roy Buchanon Collection $19.95
00690364 Cake – Songbook $19.95
00690337 Jerry Cantrell – Boggy Depot $19.95
00690293 Best of Steven Curtis Chapman $19.95
00690043 Cheap Trick – Best Of $19.95
00690171 Chicago – Definitive Guitar Collection . . . $22.95
00690393 Eric Clapton – Selections from Blues . . . $19.95
00660139 Eric Clapton – Journeyman $19.95
00694869 Eric Clapton – Live Acoustic $19.95
00694896 John Mayall/Eric Clapton – Bluesbreakers $19.95
00690162 Best of the Clash $19.95
00690166 Albert Collins – The Alligator Years $16.95
00694940 Counting Crows – August & Everything After $19.95
00690197 Counting Crows – Recovering the Satellites $19.95
00690118 Cranberries – The Best of $19.95
00690215 Music of Robert Cray $19.95
00694840 Cream – Disraeli Gears $19.95
00690352 Creed – My Own Pirson $19.95
00690007 Danzig 4 . . . . $19.95
00690184 dc Talk – Jesus Freak $19.95
00690333 dc Talk – Supernatural $19.95
00660186 Alex De Grassi Guitar Collection $19.95
00690289 Best of Deep Purple $17.95
00694831 Derek And The Dominos –
　　　　　Layla & Other Assorted Love Songs $19.95
00690322 Ani Di Franco – Little Plastic Castle $19.95
00690187 Dire Straits – Brothers In Arms $19.95
00690191 Dire Straits – Money For Nothing $24.95
00695382 The Very Best of Dire Straits –
　　　　　Sultans of Swing $19.95
00660178 Willie Dixon – Master Blues Composer . . . $24.95
00690250 Best of Duane Eddy $16.95
00690349 Eve 6 . . . . $19.95
00690323 Fastball – All the Pain Money Can Buy . . . $19.95
00690089 Foo Fighters $19.95
00690235 Foo Fighters – The Colour and the Shape . $19.95
00690394 Foo Fighters –
　　　　　There Is Nothing Left to Lose $19.95
00694920 Free – Best Of $18.95
00690324 Fuel – Sunburn $19.95
00690222 G3 Live – Satriani, Vai, Johnson $22.95

00694807 Danny Gatton – 88 Elmira St $19.95
00690127 Goo Goo Dolls – A Boy Named Goo $19.95
00690338 Goo Goo Dolls – Dizzy Up the Girl $19.95
00690117 John Gorka Collection $19.95
00690114 Buddy Guy Collection Vol. A-J $22.95
00690193 Buddy Guy Collection Vol. L-Y $22.95
00694798 George Harrison Anthology $19.95
00690068 Return Of The Hellecasters $19.95
00692930 Jimi Hendrix – Are You Experienced? $24.95
00692931 Jimi Hendrix – Axis: Bold As Love $22.95
00692932 Jimi Hendrix – Electric Ladyland $24.95
00690218 Jimi Hendrix – First Rays of the New Rising Sun $24.95
00690038 Gary Hoey – Best Of $19.95
00660029 Buddy Holly $19.95
00660169 John Lee Hooker – A Blues Legend $19.95
00690054 Hootie & The Blowfish –
　　　　　Cracked Rear View $19.95
00694905 Howlin' Wolf $19.95
00690136 Indigo Girls – 1200 Curfews $22.95
00694938 Elmore James –
　　　　　Master Electric Slide Guitar $19.95
00690167 Skip James Blues Guitar Collection $16.95
00694833 Billy Joel For Guitar $19.95
00694912 Eric Johnson – Ah Via Musicom $19.95
00690169 Eric Johnson – Venus Isle $22.95
00694799 Robert Johnson – At The Crossroads $19.95
00693185 Judas Priest – Vintage Hits $19.95
00690277 Best of Kansas $19.95
00690073 B. B. King – 1950-1957 . . . . $24.95
00690098 B. B. King – 1958-1967 . . . . $24.95
00690134 Freddie King Collection $17.95
00694903 The Best Of Kiss $24.95
00690157 Kiss – Alive $19.95
00690163 Mark Knopfler/Chet Atkins – Neck and Neck $19.95
00690296 Patty Larkin Songbook $17.95
00690070 Live – Throwing Copper $19.95
00690018 Living Colour – Best Of $19.95
00694845 Yngwie Malmsteen – Fire And Ice $19.95
00694956 Bob Marley – Legend $19.95
00690283 Best of Sarah McLachlan $19.95
00690382 Sarah McLachlan – Mirrorball $19.95
00690354 Sarah McLachlan – Surfacing $19.95
00690239 Matchbox 20 – Yourself or Someone Like You $19.95
00690244 Megadeath – Cryptic Writings $19.95
00690236 Mighty Mighty Bosstones – Let's Face It . $19.95
00690040 Steve Miller Band Greatest Hits $19.95
00694802 Gary Moore – Still Got The Blues $19.95
00694958 Mountain, Best Of $19.95
00694913 Nirvana – In Utero $19.95
00694883 Nirvana – Nevermind $19.95
00690026 Nirvana – Acoustic In New York $19.95
00690121 Oasis – (What's The Story) Morning Glory $19.95
00690290 Offspring, The – Ignition $19.95
00690204 Offspring, The – Ixnay on the Hombre . . . $17.95
00690203 Offspring, The – Smash $17.95
00694830 Ozzy Osbourne – No More Tears $19.95
00694855 Pearl Jam – Ten $19.95
00690053 Liz Phair – Whip Smart $19.95
00690176 Phish – Billy Breathes $22.95
00690331 Phish – The Story of Ghost $19.95
00693800 Pink Floyd – Early Classics $19.95
00694967 Police – Message In A Box Boxed Set $70.00
00694974 Queen – A Night At The Opera $19.95
00690395 Rage Against The Machine –
　　　　　The Battle of Los Angeles $19.95
00690145 Rage Against The Machine – Evil Empire . $19.95
00690179 Rancid – And Out Come the Wolves $22.95

00690055 Red Hot Chili Peppers –
　　　　　Bloodsugarsexmagik $19.95
00690379 Red Hot Chili Peppers – Californication . $19.95
00690090 Red Hot Chili Peppers – One Hot Minute . $22.95
00694892 Guitar Style Of Jerry Reed $19.95
00694937 Jimmy Reed – Master Bluesman $19.95
00694899 R.E.M. – Automatic For The People $19.95
00690260 Jimmie Rodgers Guitar Collection $17.95
00690014 Rolling Stones – Exile On Main Street . . . $24.95
00690186 Rolling Stones – Rock & Roll Circus $19.95
00690135 Otis Rush Collection $19.95
00690031 Santana's Greatest Hits $19.95
00694805 Scorpions – Crazy World $19.95
00690150 Son Seals – Bad Axe Blues $17.95
00690128 Seven Mary Three – American Standards . $19.95
00690076 Sex Pistols – Never Mind The Bollocks . . $19.95
00120105 Kenny Wayne Shepherd – Ledbetter Heights $19.95
00120123 Kenny Wayne Shepherd – Trouble Is $19.95
00690196 Silverchair – Freak Show $19.95
00690130 Silverchair – Frogstomp $19.95
00690041 Smithereens – Best Of $19.95
00694885 Spin Doctors – Pocket Full Of Kryptonite . $19.95
00690124 Sponge – Rotting Pinata $19.95
00694921 Steppenwolf, The Best Of $22.95
00694957 Rod Stewart – Acoustic Live $22.95
00690021 Sting – Fields Of Gold $19.95
00690242 Suede – Coming Up $19.95
00694824 Best Of James Taylor $16.95
00690238 Third Eye Blind $19.95
00690267 311 . . . . $19.95
00690030 Toad The Wet Sprocket $19.95
00690228 Tonic – Lemon Parade $19.95
00690295 Tool – Aenima $19.95
00699191 The Best of U2 – 1980-1990 . . . . $19.95
00694411 U2 – The Joshua Tree $19.95
00690039 Steve Vai – Alien Love Secrets $24.95
00690172 Steve Vai – Fire Garden $24.95
00690023 Jimmie Vaughan – Strange Pleasures $19.95
00690370 Stevie Ray Vaughan and Double Trouble –
　　　　　The Real Deal: Greatest Hits Volume 2 . $22.95
00660136 Stevie Ray Vaughan – In Step $19.95
00694835 Stevie Ray Vaughan – The Sky Is Crying . $19.95
00694776 Vaughan Brothers – Family Style $19.95
00690217 Verve Pipe, The – Villains $19.95
00120026 Joe Walsh – Look What I Did... . . . . $24.95
00694789 Muddy Waters – Deep Blues $24.95
00690071 Weezer $19.95
00690286 Weezer – Pinkerton $19.95
00694970 Who, The – Definitive Collection A-E . . . $24.95
00694971 Who, The – Definitive Collection F-Li . . . $24.95
00694972 Who, The – Definitive Collection Lo-R . . . $24.95
00694973 Who, The – Definitive Collection S-Y $24.95
00690320 Best of Dar Williams $17.95
00690319 Best of Stevie Wonder $19.95
00690319 Stevie Wonder – Some of the Best $19.95